CAMBRIDGE LIBRARY COLLECTION

Books of enduring scholarly value

History

The books reissued in this series include accounts of historical events and movements by eye-witnesses and contemporaries, as well as landmark studies that assembled significant source materials or developed new historiographical methods. The series includes work in social, political and military history on a wide range of periods and regions, giving modern scholars ready access to influential publications of the past.

Hand-book to the Naval and Military Resources of the Principal European Nations

Sir Frederick Charles Lascelles Wraxall (1828–1865) was a historian, novelist and translator (from French and German) who spent most of his short adult life in mainland Europe. Amongst his many publications was the 1862 authorised translation of Victor Hugo's *Les Miserables*. He served as assistant commissary at Kerch in the Crimea in 1856 and afterwards maintained a strong interest in military matters, on which he published several books. This volume, first published in 1856, outlines the military capability of thirteen European nations at the end of the Crimean War. Wraxall uses German military intelligence documents to describe the organisation and strength of the armies and navies of countries including Britain, France, Russia, Turkey, Prussia, Austria and Belgium. Containing detailed descriptions of the numbers of infantry, cavalry, engineers, artillery, ships and crew for each country, the book remains a valuable resource for military historians interested in mid-nineteenth-century Europe.

Cambridge University Press has long been a pioneer in the reissuing of out-of-print titles from its own backlist, producing digital reprints of books that are still sought after by scholars and students but could not be reprinted economically using traditional technology. The Cambridge Library Collection extends this activity to a wider range of books which are still of importance to researchers and professionals, either for the source material they contain, or as landmarks in the history of their academic discipline.

Drawing from the world-renowned collections in the Cambridge University Library, and guided by the advice of experts in each subject area, Cambridge University Press is using state-of-the-art scanning machines in its own Printing House to capture the content of each book selected for inclusion. The files are processed to give a consistently clear, crisp image, and the books finished to the high quality standard for which the Press is recognised around the world. The latest print-on-demand technology ensures that the books will remain available indefinitely, and that orders for single or multiple copies can quickly be supplied.

The Cambridge Library Collection will bring back to life books of enduring scholarly value (including out-of-copyright works originally issued by other publishers) across a wide range of disciplines in the humanities and social sciences and in science and technology.

Hand-book to the Naval and Military Resources of the Principal European Nations

LASCELLES WRAXALL

CAMBRIDGE
UNIVERSITY PRESS

CAMBRIDGE UNIVERSITY PRESS

Cambridge, New York, Melbourne, Madrid, Cape Town, Singapore,
São Paolo, Delhi, Dubai, Tokyo, Mexico City

Published in the United States of America by Cambridge University Press, New York

www.cambridge.org
Information on this title: www.cambridge.org/9781108026505

© in this compilation Cambridge University Press 2010

This edition first published 1856
This digitally printed version 2010

ISBN 978-1-108-02650-5 Paperback

HAND-BOOK

TO

THE NAVAL AND MILITARY RESOURCES

OF THE

Principal European Nations.

HAND-BOOK

TO THE

NAVAL AND MILITARY RESOURCES

OF THE

Principal European Nations.

BY

LASCELLES WRAXALL,

ASSISTANT COMMISSARY, FIELD TRAIN, TURKISH CONTINGENT.

LONDON

W. AND R. CHAMBERS, 47, PATERNOSTER ROW,

AND HIGH STREET, EDINBURGH.

MDCCCLVI.

PREFACE.

THE very favourable reception accorded to some papers on the Armies of Germany, which I recently published in the *New Monthly Magazine* (and a portion of which has been incorporated with the present work), induced me to pursue my researches further. The result has been the little work which I now venture to present to the public.

I do not believe any remark is necessary, on my part, as to the selection of the states to which I have directed my attention. Denmark, Belgium, and Holland, owing to their position near and between Great Powers, could not be passed over, as they are compelled by that position to take a voluntary or involuntary part in every general European war.

The principal sources whence I have derived my information are the excellent military papers of Germany. Strange to say, our own army caused me more labour than all the rest; but Mr Thompson's recently published and valuable work afforded me very welcome assistance.

In a book of this nature, it is impossible to prevent some slight errors; but I have used my utmost endeavours to secure accuracy, and I confidently trust that I have been successful.

Note by the Publishers.—This work having passed through the press while the author was absent on professional duty, it is possible that some typographical errors may have been overlooked. For these, in consideration of the circumstances, the indulgence of the reader is requested.

TABLE OF CONTENTS.

INTRODUCTION.

It must seem probable to every one who pays the slightest attention to passing events, that we are as yet merely on the threshold of a great European war, destined to decide the fate of continental Europe. Through our insular position, we may regard ourselves as safe from many of those contingencies which may arise; but through that very fact it becomes the more our duty to use our utmost endeavours to keep the Russian Czar within the limits of his own empire, and not permit him longer to extend his territory after the fashion introduced by Catherine II., and so pertinaciously persevered in by her successors.

The conduct of the Austrian and Prussian monarchs must shew us how firmly the Emperor of Russia has founded an *imperium in imperio* upon Teutonic soil. With marvellous patience we have continued to wait for a decided movement on the part of Austria; and that movement, when it came at last, has disappointed us egregiously. It is quite certain that, until a pressure of circumstances impel her to action, she will continue passive towards Russia. She has planted herself firmly in the Principalities, and we

A

can imagine her chuckling inwardly over the idea
that she has swallowed the oyster, while we are con-
tending for the shells. Of course, neither England
nor France can allow such occupation to be permanent ; but the ousting her may be attended with very
great difficulty.

Prussia, on the other hand, has behaved in a more
decided fashion. From the first outbreak of the war,
it was clear that the king would never consent to
aid us against his brother-in-law ; and, though the
wishes of the people may be with us, unfortunately
their voice is but slightly heard in a country kept
down by an armed *soldateska*. Great jealousy of
Austria has also done much to prevent Prussia openly
siding with either party ; but it may now be expected
that, as the king has no reason to conceal his policy
longer, he will soon avow his predilection, and openly
declare himself an ally of our Russian foe. The un-
expected resistance we met with at Sevastopol has
done much to lower our *prestige* in Germany ; and
even now that the dread fortress has fallen, a strong
sense of the difficulty of our task remains.

In any long-continued war, England will infallibly
be compelled to have recourse to subsidising foreign
troops ; and the question naturally is, where these
may be obtained. On this subject we have a crotchet,
which we venture to make known, leaving our read-
ers to estimate its value.

Napoleon the First, although master of armies to
which ours appear but Lilliputian, was, nevertheless,
compelled to seek assistance from without. He
founded the Rhenish Confederation, and so obtained a
very large amount of support. Are circumstances so

altered, that the Third Napoleon should despair of success in trying the same experiment? In point of progress, Germany is the same now as it was fifty years ago. The same jealousies exist among the smaller princes, and each would sell the other at a moment's notice, if any material advantage could be derived from it. Bavaria is still smarting from the loss of the Palatinate; and her assistance, by means of a large and well-disciplined army, would be cheaply purchased by lopping Baden of some of her ill-acquired territory. Saxony, again, has not forgotten the iniquitous partition of the Congress of Vienna; and a promise of revenge would be a mighty lever to set her armies in motion. In what do 1808 and 1855 so greatly differ, that we might not purchase (it's an ugly word, but the real one) the valuable assistance of troops now wasting their energies in acting as policemen, and putting down beer commotions? Those mistaken notions, which appear to have sprung up from a morbid desire of peace at any price, have hitherto caused us to refrain from drawing other nations into the contest, forgetting the while that their vitality is imperilled more than our own. We certainly take the goods the gods provide us; and, when a Quixotic monarch offers us his troops *gratis*, and we lend him a couple of millions in the same disinterested fashion, we feel as if we had done a good stroke of business. But such is not the way in which a war, more especially with Russia, must be carried on. Necessity will compel us, ere long, to count up our friends, whether interested or disinterested; and the longer we delay, the greater will be the price we shall have to pay.

We are not singular in these views, as will be seen by an extract we purpose to make from a paper published at Stockholm, called the *Svenska Tidningen:*—

"Now that the sun of spring is beginning to melt our snow, and burst the ice which enchains our seas, the Western Powers will assuredly renew their appeals to the Northern States to join their alliance. Will they succeed? Will the King of Sweden and Norway, who, by the fundamental laws, alone has right to declare war, break the neutrality he has hitherto maintained? This is a question of immense importance for the future of our country, which our governments must face in the midst of difficulties, dangers, and caprice. The Western Powers have already attached Sardinia to their cause; she has sent 15,000 men to the Eastern seat of war. The same Powers are striving to gain Portugal, which can only offer them a still smaller number of troops. If England and France are seeking such allies, what advantages would they derive from having Sweden and Norway on their side, able to throw *very much more considerable forces* on the side of the Baltic? Our assistance would be of especial service to England, when she possesses at this moment no army to send to the Baltic, nor can she form one; and in our flotilla she would find that species of maritime arm so necessary for crippling the Russians. France, too, would have 60,000 men at her disposition, whom, in the event of our non-assistance, she would be compelled to send to the north.

"Our situation is not that of Sardinia or Portugal, although there is some resemblance between the population and military forces. We are not, like them, at a great distance from the seat of war ; we are not, like Sardinia, enclosed between two great protecting powers ; nor, like Portugal, situate at the extremity of Europe, under the ægis of an imposing flag. Our situation has more analogy with that of Austria. Like her, we are close to the great enemy, far from our great allies; we should be the *first*, and probably the *last*, to bear the burden of the war. Austria, who can bring into the field 200,000 men, for whom the present war is a vital question, as her most precious commercial advantages, her religious and political independence are at stake,—Austria, who has on her right Turkey for an ally, and on her left France, ready to send a formidable army to her aid through Germany, — Austria hesitates about drawing the sword, and is using her utmost exertions to terminate the contest by negotiations ; and we, for whom the famous Four Points present scarce any interest—for whom the war has no settled object—are expected to hurl ourselves into it blindly !

" We say that the war has no definite object as far as we are concerned. But would not the weakening of Russia be of great effect on the future of Sweden ? Doubtlessly, if this weakening is brought about. But the Great Powers are not yet agreed on this point. What resolutions have been formed ? As long as the question remains as it is, we are on a sea of uncertainty. As long as the Great Powers have not agreed on a definitive settlement of the European balance, our union with them in the Russian war would only be a support given to a policy full of chances impossible to foresee, and of no advantage to us. We cannot afford to run so great a risk.

" No ; before the three Great Powers at least have
decided resolutely to deprive Russia of important
territories, we do not believe that Sweden ought to
give up that state of peace and security which she
enjoys at present—a *status* recognised by the whole
of Europe, even by Russia, and blessed by the peoples
of the united kingdoms. It is not yet known, and
probably we shall not be informed for some time, how
far the Allies have resolved to dismember Russia.
Even if Austria were to give the Allies that armed
co-operation for which they have waited so long, it
would not then be certain that this dismemberment
would be declared a necessary condition of peace.
Might not other means be found which would equally
satisfy the honour of all parties ?—and where should
we be in such a case ? "

The arguments employed by the Swedes are good,
and may be applied equally to Germany. Unless we
can offer the smaller German princes a guarantee that
they run no risk, it would be difficult to induce them
to join us. Such guarantee could be afforded by
a French army on the Rhine. The real truth is,
Austria *dare not* engage in the contest. At the present moment she is compelled to send Radetzky very
considerable reinforcements ; for the whole of Italy is
smouldering, and the fire may burst forth at any
point. Hungary is quiet, it is true, but Poland will
yet be a thorn in the side of her oppressors ; and we
believe that there is nothing to prevent our obtaining
the assistance of the smaller German princes if we
like to bid for it. The great bugbear of Russian
influence is decidedly exaggerated. The princes may
be on the side of the Czar, but the people are not : and

the military in these states are very different from the Austrian *soldateska*. Owing to the poverty of the governments, the troops are constantly on furlough ; and hence a feeling of fraternisation with the people is largely kept up. 1848 taught us what dependence the smaller regents could place in their troops ; and we feel confident that, were we to make a bid, the English government could secure the whole of Southern Germany to their side. It is not our business to point out the rewards that should be offered—we leave these to abler heads than our own ; but one effect of our present labours will be to show where a very large accession of strength may be acquired. If the proper measures are taken, a foreign legion may be easily obtained, far superior to the specimens now to be seen at Heligoland and Shorncliffe.

I.

THE BRITISH FORCES.

BRITISH ARMY—INDIAN ARMY.

BRITISH NAVY—INDIAN NAVY.

THE BRITISH ARMY

Is divided into two separate and independent portions —the Royal or British, and the East Indian Army.

THE ROYAL ARMY

Is composed of (1.) the Standing Army, to which infantry and cavalry belong; (2.) the Ordnance, comprising artillery, engineers, and *matériel;* and (3.) the Militia.

ADMINISTRATION AT HEAD-QUARTERS.

The Commander-in-Chief has under him—

(1.) The infantry and cavalry; (2.) the staff-officers; (3.) the clothing board; (4.) the medical department; (5.) the home military districts; (6.) the veterinary surgeons; (7.) military schools, hospitals, depôts, &c.; (8.) the recruiting districts.

Head-quarters' staff consists of the personal and army staffs. There are three offices at head-quarters:—(1.) Purchase of commissions, promotion of officers, and organisation of the army; (2.) pay and petitions; (3.) private correspondence between the Commander-in-Chief and the Government; and three departments:—(1.) Adjutant-General's department, with one Lieutenant-General—substitution, remounts,

clothing, arming, recruiting, and discharging, &c.;
(2.) Quartermaster-General's department—dislocation,
quartering, encamping, billeting and cantonment,
marches and reliefs; finally, (3.) the Medical department.

The English army has neither an adjutancy nor a
general staff like the majority of European armies, as
the officers appointed to such duties are taken from
the regiments, in which their promotion goes on just
the same.

There are five ranks of general officers in the British service:—(1.) field-marshals, (2.) generals, (3.)
lieutenant-generals, (4.) major-generals, (5.) brigadier-generals.

The staff-officers:—official and personal staff, garrison and recruiting staff. The official staff contains the
adjutant-generals, officers of the quartermaster-general's staff, and majors of brigade. The personal staff
consists of the aides-de-camp and military secretaries.
The garrison staff comprises the town-majors, adjutants, &c. Lastly, the recruiting staff contains the
staff-officers inspecting recruits, adjutants, surgeons,
paymasters, &c., required for that branch of the service.

England is divided into six military districts, the
commanders of which are usually generals. Their
functions tally with those of the general commanders
of other armies, and consist in inspecting the regiments in their district, as well as embarkation and
debarkation of troops; the military resources of the
district, and available means of defence, &c. In
the same way Great Britain is divided into nine
recruiting districts, with the necessary subdivisions.

THE ORDNANCE.

The Master-General of the Ordnance has several departments under him:—The artillery, the engineers, the sappers and miners, the train ; the medical, administrative, and barrack *personnel* of the ordnance; the 16 ordnance, and 29 barrack districts; various military establishments (arsenal at Woolwich, magazine at Waltham Abbey, the artillery and engineers' schools, &c.); organisation and distribution of the ordnance troops ; the construction of fortifications and military buildings, the surveys, &c.

WAR DEPARTMENT.

Since the commencement of the Russian War, the War and Colonial Departments have been separated; and the administration of the former is now under the care of the *Secretary of State for the War Department*, or, briefly, the War Minister; while the old office of Secretary-at-War is also kept up. The War Minister is the administrative head of the army, and makes known to the Commander-in-Chief the Cabinet decisions with regard to the amount of military force to be annually maintained ; settles the distribution of these forces, and plans campaigns. All changes in the organisation of the army—in the system of pay, promotion, &c.—emanate from him, as the representative of royal authority. The economy and finance of the army — pay, clothing, and commissariat; chaplains, the medical department (in conjunction with the Commander-in-Chief), military justice, and the enforcement of the civil law when violated by military men—all come within the range of his authority.

The militia, yeomanry, and pensioners, are under the control of the Home Secretary, who is responsible for the internal defence of the country.

Owing to the strength of the military resources of Britain being annually decided by Parliament, it is difficult to give any accurate account of them. The army is composed of native and colonial troops, militia, and pensioners; and is not divided into *corps d'armée;* these which have to be formed on the outbreak of a war.

HOME AND COLONIAL TROOPS.

1. *Infantry.*

This branch of the service is divided into line, light infantry, and rifles; 3 guard regiments; 98 line, fusilier, and light regiments; 1 rifle corps, 1 rifle brigade, and 1 depôt battalion of home; 7 line regiments, and 1 invalid depôt of colonial infantry.

HOME INFANTRY.

Foot Guards.
{ 1 regiment Grenadier Guards, of 3 battalions and 32 companies; 96 commissioned officers and 2902 men.
1 regiment Coldstream Guards, and 1 Scotch Fusiliers, each 2 battalions, 20 companies, 1600 rank and file; 61 officers—127 non-commissioned and commissioned each.

The household brigade thus consists of 3 regiments, 7 battalions, and 6748 soldiers, including officers and men.

Each regiment is commanded by a colonel, lieutenant-colonel, with a surgeon-major; each battalion, by a major, with a surgeon and his assistants; lastly, each company, by a captain, one or more lieutenants, and an ensign. The guards have higher rank and pay than the other troops (a lieutenant, guards = cap-

tain in the army, &c.), but their armament, &c., resembles that of the line.

Line Infantry.	1 regiment (1st), of two battalions, of 10 companies each. 2 regiments (12th and 91st), of two battalions, 6 companies each. 82 regiments, of one battalion, of 10 companies.	85 regiments, or 88 battalions; 87,902 men.

The ordinary strength of a regiment of infantry, of
a single battalion, is 750; or, where there are two,
1250. By the last estimates, each battalion will be
raised to 1000 rank and file, excepting the 12th regiment, which reckons 1200.

One line infantry battalion is generally divided into
10 companies, each having a captain, lieutenant, and
ensign, or 2 lieutenants; there are, however, generally 13 lieutenants, and from 8 to 10 ensigns in each
regiment. It is also commanded by a colonel, lieutenant-colonel, and two majors; with a staff made up
of an adjutant, lieutenant-quartermaster, paymaster,
surgeon, and assistant-surgeon. The number of
commissioned officers is generally 40. The troops
are armed with Minié rifles and bayonets.

Fusiliers.	1 regiment (23d), of 2 battalions each, 6 companies. 4 regiments (5th, 7th, 21st, 87th), of 1 battalion, 10 companies.	
Light Infantry.	1 regiment (71st), of 2 battalions of 10 companies. 7 regiments (13th, 43d, 51st, 52d, 68th, 85th, 90th), of 1 battalion of 10 companies.	13 regiments, or 20 light battalions of 19,500 men.
Rifles.	60th regiment, of 2 battalions of 10 companies. 1 rifle brigade—3 battalions of 10 companies.	

These regiments are officered like the other regiments of the line, and armed with Minié and Brunswick rifles.

COLONIAL INFANTRY.

3 West Indian regiments of 2 battalions and 6 companies.
1 St Helena regiment of 2 battalions and 5 companies.
1 Canadian Rifle corps of 6 companies.
1 Gold Coast corps of 3 companies.
1 Ceylon Rifle regiment of 9 companies.
1 Fencible regiment (Malta), 6 companies.
Newfoundland corps, 3 companies.

} 7 regiments, and 6 Companies = 7906 men.

Armament : like the infantry.

Hence, the strength of the entire infantry may be estimated at 110 regiments, or 126 battalions = 121,994 men, which is (October 1855) daily being increased.

2. *Cavalry.*

13 regiments of light, and 13 regiments heavy cavalry, exclusive of the 12 companies of mounted rifles (colonial cavalry).

HOME CAVALRY.

Heavy Cavalry. {
3 Guard regiments (2d Life Guards and 1 Horse Guards).
9 Heavy Dragoon regiments (7th Dragoon Guards).
1 Carbineer regiment.

Light Cavalry. {
4 Light Dragoon regiments.
4 Lancer regiments.
5 Hussar regiments.

Total strength of cavalry :—26 regiments = 12,460 men, with 9,396 horses.

The distinction between light and heavy cavalry consists, rather in the name and uniform, than in the size of men and horses, &c.

The Guards have higher pay and rank.

Each regiment of cavalry comprises a colonel, lieutenant-colonel, major, 6 captains, and 13 subalterns, with the regimental staff, amounting to 27 officers. On a war footing, there are 2 lieutenant-colonels, 2 majors, 9 captains, and 26 subaltern officers. The strength of the non-commissioned officers and troopers varies from 304 to 628 men, with 271 to 704 horses.

COLONIAL CAVALRY (CAPE OF GOOD HOPE).

12 companies of mounted rifles, with 900 horses, and about 1100 men.

Total strength of the English cavalry :—26 regiments and 12 companies, about 13,600 men, with 10,300 horses.

ARTILLERY.

The English artillery is divided into the Royal Artillery and the brigade of Royal Horse Artillery.

The artillery is divided into field batteries, mountain-batteries, and colonial batteries, the two first containing light and heavy guns. The field-batteries consist of 6 guns (5 guns and 1 howitzer); the 18-pounder batteries, however, have 4 guns (3 guns and 1 howitzer). The colonial and mountain batteries are each composed of 3 guns and $4\frac{2}{3}$-inch cohorn mortar. Each battery has a rocket detachment attached to it.

B

(1.) The   ⌠ 12 battalions, of 8 companies or batteries.
Royal   ⎥   1 detachment African artillery (Jamaica).
Artillery   ⎨   1 company gun lascars (Hong Kong).
Regiment.   ⎣   1   „   invalids.

A battery is generally made up of 6 officers, 11 ⎤
non-commissioned officers, and 90 gunners.   ⎥ 10 artizans.
    Train—1 officer, 9 to 18 non-commissioned ⎟
    officers—73 to 102 drivers.   ⎦
    Horses — 6-pounder light battery, 143 ; 9-pounder bat-
    tery, 164 ; 12-pounder do., 198, including 8 baggage
    horses.

The regiment—1 colonel (Master of Ordnance), 184 staff-officers ; 60 adjutants, quartermasters, surgeons, &c. ; 448
officers, 1152 non-commissioned officers, 11,954 gunners and
drivers.

The detachment in Jamaica contains 61, the company in Hong
Kong 88, and the invalid company 145 men.

(2.) Brigade ⎛ 7 companies, or batteries⎞ 695 men, 492 horses
of Horse   ⎨ 1 company   or   battery ⎬   (peace establish-
Artillery,   ⎝   (rocket).   ⎠   ment).

1 Battery   ⎫ 6-pounder—6 officers, 18 non-commissioned offi-
(war estab· ⎬   cers, 149 gunners, 9 artizans, 186 horses.
lishment). ⎭

    9-pounder—6 officers, 20 non-commissioned offi-
    cers, 170 gunners, 11 artizans, 220 horses.

    1 rocket section—2 non-commissioned officers,
    10 gunners, 10 horses.

(Each horse battery has a rocket section attached.)

The brigade (peace establishment)—1 colonel commanding,
6 staff officers, 5 adjutants, 1 quartermaster, surgeons, &c. ;
7 staff sergeants, 35 officers, 70 non-commissioned officers,
571 trumpeters, gunners, drivers, and artizans.

In addition, the following corps are attached to
the artillery :—1 riding-house troop of 3 officers, 6
non-commissioned officers, 25 rough-riders ; and the
field-train department, consisting of 7 officers, a medical department of 47 surgeons, &c.

Total strength of the English artillery = 103 companies, or 15,122 men.

ENGINEERS

are divided into the corps of Royal Engineers and the Sappers and Miners.

(1.) The engineers consist of about 280 officers, the master-general as colonel, 6 colonels-commandant, 12 colonels, 30 lieutentant-colonels, 48 captains, 48 second captains, 96 first lieutenants, 36 second lieutenants, an inspector-general of fortifications, with a first and second assistant, and an assistant adjutant-general.

(2.) Sappers and Miners. { 23 companies, 1 brigade major, 1 adjutant, 1 quartermaster, 247 staff sergeants and non-commissioned officers, 64 musicians, 1791 men. } 2185 men.

Total strength of the active English army = 147,089 men, with 120 horsed guns.

MILITIA AND PENSIONERS.

The strength of the militia has recently been raised to 120,000 men—80,000 for England, 10,000 for Scotland, and 30,000 for Ireland, with 3271 officers. There are 82 English, 17 Scotch, and 41 Irish regiments embodied; but the total number of rank and file, at the present time, does not amount to 70,000 men. The regiments are generally filled up by recruiting; but, if these means fail, recourse will be had to the ballot, for all between the ages of 17 and 25. The time of service lasts five years, and the troops can be called out to exercise for from 3 to 56 days. The government provides arms and uniform; and, during the period of being on duty, the militia are placed on a footing with the regular army.

The officers are appointed partly by the Secretary for the Home Department, partly by the Lord-Lieutenant of the county. Formerly, the militia could not be called upon to serve abroad; but, by a recent Act, they can now be taken to the Colonies, &c.

The dockyard battalions, formed of volunteers among the superintendents, clerks, and workmen of the naval establishments, are 10 in number, with an effective strength of about 10,000 men.

The volunteers amount to about 14,000 or 15,000 men, divided into 52 corps. They are generally yeomanry cavalry. Time of service each year—14 days.

The pensioners are composed of all those retired soldiers who may still be called on to serve; they are called out annually for 14 days' training, and number 18,500 men, 2000 of them serving in the colonies.

MILITARY SCHOOLS.

Military academy at Woolwich—military institution at Sandhurst—engineers' school at Chatham—artillery, sappers and miners' school at Woolwich—the riding-school at Maidstone—regimental schools attached to each regiment for the sons and daughters of soldiers, as well as for non-commissioned officers, &c.

REMARKS.—The complement of the English army is kept up by enlistment of men between the ages of 17 and 25, for 10 to 12 years (the latter time for horse artillery and cavalry) ; promotion by distinguished services in the field or during peace (recently allowed to non-commissioned officers) ; seniority ; and purchase, from lieutenant-colonel downwards (cadets, royal pages, and sons of distinguished statesmen, appointed without payment). All the commissions in the ordnance department are given without purchase, as well as those vacated by death or removal. Lately, a slight examination for officers has been introduced ; mobilization of the English army, without any divided *cadre* or depôt divisions, as a portion of each regiment is always left at home.

THE EAST INDIAN ARMY.

The British army in the East Indies consists of European and native troops. To the former belong royal troops, and those enlisted by the East India Company at home ; and the native troops are divided into regular and irregular. This army is under the supreme command of the Governor of the East Indies, and is divided into 3 corps—the armies of Madras, Bombay, and Bengal. The regiments are organised like those of the British army.

1. ROYAL TROOPS.

25 infantry and 5 cavalry regiments, with a strength of 31,000 men, paid by the East India Company, and relieved every twenty years. Owing to

the fatiguing service and dangerous climate, these
troops enjoy special privileges.

2. EUROPEAN TROOPS.

6 regiments of infantry, of 10 companies, including 2 light regiments	6,100 men.
12 battalions of 16 companies foot artillery, each company about 100 men . . .	6,800 „
5 brigades of 17 batteries horse artillery, each battery about 116 men	
Engineers, about	200 „
Total . .	13,100 men.

Organisation and armament like the royal troops—
which is also the case with the regular native regiments.

3. NATIVE TROOPS.

(1.) *Regular Troops.*

135 regiments infantry	= about	186,000 men.
21 „ cavalry	= „	10,900 „
6 battalions horse } artillery,	= „	3,800 „
6 „ foot }		
Sappers and miners		2,600 „
Total . .		203,300 men.

(2.) *Irregular Troops.*

About 33 regiments infantry, 30 regiments cavalry,
several batteries and sapper companies, as well as
police battalions = about 60,000 men.

In organisation, uniform, and armament, they differ
greatly from the other regiments. Thus, for instance,
they have a so-called Camel Brigade.

The contingent supplied by the dependent native

princes may be estimated at 40,000 men, but no great confidence can be placed in them.

Total strength of the East Indian army—about 320,000 men.

The troops contained in sections 2 and 3 are distributed as follows :—

ARMY OF MADRAS.

Infantry—2 European and 52 native regiments.
Cavalry—8 light regiments.

Artillery,
1 regiment.
$$\begin{cases} 1 \text{ brigade horse artillery} = 4 \text{ European and 4} \\ \quad \text{native batteries.} \\ 4 \text{ battalions European foot artillery} = 16 \text{ com-} \\ \quad \text{panies.} \\ 1 \text{ battalion of native foot artillery} = 6 \text{ companies.} \end{cases}$$

1 European infantry regiment contains—1 colonel, 2 lieutenant-colonels, 2 majors, 12 captains, 12 first, and 10 second lieutenants.

1 native infantry regiment contains—1 colonel, 1 lieutenant-colonel, 1 major, 6 captains, 10 first-lieutenants, and 5 ensigns.

1 cavalry regiment contains—1 colonel, 1 lieutenant-colonel, 6 captains, 8 lieutenants, and 4 cornets.

1 artillery regiment contains—1 colonel, 1 lieutenant-colonel, 7 majors, 35 captains, 70 first, and 35 second lieutenants.

Engineer corps—46 officers.

These data may be referred to the other two armies.

ARMY OF BOMBAY.

Infantry—2 European and 29 native regiments.
Cavalry—3 regiments.

Artillery, 1 regiment. $\begin{cases} \text{1 horse brigade} = \text{4 batteries.} \\ \text{2 batteries European artillery} = \text{4 companies.} \\ \text{2 \quad ,, \quad native artillery} = \text{6 companies.} \\ \text{Engineer corps—46 officers.} \end{cases}$

ARMY OF BENGAL.

Infantry—2 European and 74 native regiments.

Cavalry—10 regiments.

1 horse-battery $=$ 3 European and 2 native batteries.

Artillery—2 and 3-horse brigades, each 3 European and 1 native battery.

6 battalions foot artillery, each 4 companies (European) ; 3 do. do., each 6 companies (native).

Engineers—92 officers.

REMARKS.—In European Company's troops, the officers are selected from the military establishment at Addiscombe, or without purchase. Promotion to general's rank is in the hands of the English Government. In the native regiments, native and European officers serve together, and the former can advance to major. Enlistment of volunteers from 20 to 30 years of age. In case of need, the infantry is drawn from Hindus — the cavalry from Mohammedans. The baggage-train is excessively heavy (each officer having from 20 to 30 servants), and hence the army is difficult of locomotion.

THE BRITISH NAVY.

The Board of Admiralty, composed of the Admiralty and the Admiralty Court, forms the supreme marine authority.

The Admiralty—first lord, as supreme director of the administration; 3 admirals, 2 captains, 2 secretaries, and 16 civil officers.

Departments—1. Surveyor of the navy.
      2. Engineering and architectural.
      3. Victualling and transport.
      4. Accountant-general.
      5. Storekeeper.
      6. Sanitary.
Attached—7. Hydrographical and harbour department, and the Royal Marine and General Register Offices.

The fleet is divided into 3 squadrons—of the red, white, and blue ensigns. The eldest rear-admiral of the blue is promoted to be youngest rear-admiral of the white, &c.

PERSONNEL OF FLEET, APRIL 1855.

OFFICERS.

	Normal Strength.	Effective.	Active.	Hf.-pay.	Pension.
Fleet Admirals ...	1	1	1	0	0
Flag „ ...	21	34	21	6	7
Vice „ ...	27	41	27	12	2
Rear „ ...	51	207	51	31	125
Captains............	350	652	252	220	180
Lieutenants	1200	1952	1022	915	15
Masters, 1st Class	0	432	119	313	0
Mates	0	315	309	6	0
Masters, 2d Class	0	157	157	0	0
Engineers...........	0	96	94	0	2
Medical Officers ...	0	895	845	0	50
Clerks..............	0	708	376	113	219
Chaplains	0	128	62	66	
Instructors.........	0	69	68	0	0
Cadets	Number uncertain.				

MEN.

Seamen. { 25,541 midshipmen, petty officers, and men.
         { 2,000 boys.

Infantry, 110 companies, each of 105 men } Together about
Artillery, 12   „   „   172   „   } 1300 men, without officers.

The officers of marines are—

	Effective.	Active.	Half-pay.	Pension.
Generals..............	1	1	0	0
General officers....	62	29	1	32
Subalterns	703	374	257	72
Staff, &c.	36	36	0	0

Coast-guard, with a staff of officers, as follows :—

  2 Comptrollers-general.
 56 Inspecting commanders.   } All on
  3 Lieutenant commanders   half-pay,
196 Lieutenants.   or pen-
 42 Masters, 1st class.   sioned, as
  8   „   2d   „   are the
  8 Lieutenants of marine artillery and marines,   men
    &c.   also.
 43 Other officers.

Royal naval coast-volunteers, in 6 divisions.

Hence, the usual strength of the English sailors and marines would be about 45,000 men, though, at the present time, it is largely increased.

THE FLEET.

Rated ships—that is to say, ships registered on the list of the Royal Navy—are entered under one of the 6 following rates :—

First rates, to comprise all ships carrying 110 guns and upwards, or whose complement consists of 950 men or more.

Second rates, to comprise one of her Majesty's yachts, and all ships carrying under 110 guns, and not less than 80 guns; or whose complements are under 950, and not less than 750 men.

Third rates, to comprise her Majesty's other yachts, and all such vessels as may bear the flag or pennant of any admiral, superintendent, or captain-superintendent of one of her Majesty's dockyards; and all ships carrying under 80 guns, and not less than 70; or whose complements are under 750, and not less than 620 men.

Fourth rates, to comprise all ships carrying under 70 guns, and not less than 50; or whose complements are under 620, and not less than 450 men.

Fifth rates, to comprise all ships under 50 guns, and not less than 30; or whose complements are under 450, and not less than 300 men.

Sixth rates, to consist of all other ships bearing a captain.

Sloops to comprise bomb-ships, and all other vessels commanded by commanders.

All other ships commanded by lieutenants, and having complements of not less than 60 men.

Smaller vessels, not classed as above, to have such smaller complements as the Lords Commissioners of the Admiralty may decide.

According to the Navy List of April 1854, England has 545 vessels, either in commission or partially equipped, which may be divided as follows:—

| Rank | SAILING SHIPS | | | | SCREW STEAMERS | | | | | | PADDLE-WHEEL STEAMERS | | | | |
| | Equipped | | Building | | Equipped | | | Building | | | Equipped | | | Building | |
	No.	Guns.	No.	Guns.	No.	Guns.	H.-Power	No.	Guns.	H.-Pwr.	No.	Guns.	H.-Power	No.	H.-Pwr.
131	0	0	0	0	1	131	700	0	0	0					
120	10	1200	2	240	3	360	1700	1	120	800					
110	3	348	2	232	0	0	0	0	0	0					
100	7	723	0	0	2	201	1400	1	100	800					
90	5	450	0	0	13	1176	6600	4	360	2400					
80	23	1884	3	240	1	80	400	0	0	0					
70	22	1622	0	0	1	70	350	0	0	0					
60	3	180	3	180	4	240	1800	7	350	3200					
50	31	1530	4	200	9	452	3960	0	0	0					
40	41	1736	0	0	1	46	300	0	0	0					
30	3	110	0	0	4	128	1530	0	0	0					
20	23	575	0	0	7	149	2520	3	60	1150	3	71	1760		
10	55	751	0	0	13	193	2572	2	32	200	7	112	3170		
Under 10.	49	268	0	0	17	102	2522	2	16	110	72	335	19074	1	600
Unarmed.	26	0	0	0	1	0	120	0	0	0	31	0	3816		
Total	301	11397	14	1092	77	3328	26474	20	1038	8660	113	518	27820	1	600

Total strength:—491 ships of war, with 15,243 guns and 54,294 horse-power; further, 35 ships of war, with 2130 guns and 9260 horse-power, building; without counting 20 to 30 gun-boats, of light draught, of from 100 to 160 horse-power, and 3 to 7 guns.

At the present time, more than half these vessels are fully equipped, while the others, in ordinary, could be got ready within two to four weeks, in case the crews could be made up, which would require above 150,000 men.

In addition, we may mention—about 113 tenders, 19 guard ships, &c.; 17 revenue cutters; and from 150 to 200 large steamers, belonging to private companies, which the Government can take up in case of need.

As regards the description of ships, we find the following divisions :—

94 SHIPS OF THE LINE, of which

73 are sailing,
21 „ screw, vessels.

EQUIPPED.

6 ships of the line, of	120 guns	=	720 guns.
1 ship „	116 „	=	116 „
2 ships „	104 „	=	208 „
1 ship „	100 „	=	100 „
6 ships „	90 „	=	540 „
3 „ „	80 „	=	240 „
3 „ „	72 „	=	216 „

Total—22 ships of the line; 2140 guns.

IN ORDINARY.

3 ships of the line, of 120 guns	=	360 guns.
5 „ „ 104 „	=	520 „
10 „ „ 90 „	=	900 „
13 „ „ 80 „	=	1040 „
13 „ „ 72 „	=	936 „

44 ships of the line, with 3756 guns.

The total amount of ships equipped and in ordinary is, therefore, 66, with 5896 guns.

BUILDING.

2 ships of the line, of 120 guns,	=	240 guns.
2 „ „ 116 „	=	232 „
3 „ „ 80 „	=	240 „

92 FRIGATES, of which

68 are sailing ships,
24 „ screw steamers.

EQUIPPED.

4 frigates, of 50 guns	=	200 guns.
1 frigate, 44 „	=	44 „
3 frigates, 42 „	=	126 „
1 frigate, 40 „	=	40 „
1 „ 36 „	=	36 „

Or 10 frigates, with 446 guns.

IN ORDINARY.

23 frigates, of	50 guns		=	1150	guns.
11 ,,	44 ,,		=	484	,,
18 ,,	42 ,,		=	756	,,
4 ,,	40 ,,		=	160	,,
2 ,,	36 ,,		=	72	,,

Or 58 frigates, with 2622 guns.

The total number of frigates, equipped and in ordinary, is, consequently, 68 frigates, with 3068 guns.

CORVETTES.

45, with 914 guns. Among them, 2 of 28, 13 of 26, &c.

BRIGS, SCHOONERS, ETC.

107, with 800 guns.

PADDLE-WHEEL STEAMERS,

Including brigs, &c., 115. Of these, 80 are armed with 424 guns. Among them, 1 with 28, 2 of 26, 6 of 16, 37 of 6 guns, &c.

SCREW SHIPS OF THE LINE.

1 screw ship of the line, 700 horse-power and 130 guns.							
2 ,,	,,	500	,,	,,	121	,,
1 ,,	,,	600	,,	,,	120	,,
1 ,,	,,	600	,,	,,	100	,,
6 ,,	,,	500	,,	,,	90	,,
2 ,,	,,	450	,,	,,	80	,,
1 ,,	,,	350	,,	,,	70	,,

Or 13 screw ships of the line, with 1240 guns.

BUILDING.

2 screw ships of the line, 700 h.-p. 130 guns = 260 guns.
1 „   ship   „   600 „   100   „ = 100 „
6 „   ships   „   500 „   90   „ = 540 „

STEAM FRIGATES AND CORVETTES.

EQUIPPED.

2 screw frigates, of 60 guns   =   120 guns.
2   „   58 „   =   116 „
2   „   50 „   =   100 „
1   „   47 „   =   47   „
1   „   34 „   =   34   „
1   „   30 „   =   30   „
4   „   24 „   =   96   „
Or 13 screw frigates, with 543 guns.

There are 24 screw corvettes—some 18, some 14 guns, &c. &c.; altogether, 197 guns.

BUILDING.

3 screw frigates, of 60 guns   =   180 guns.
8   „   „ 50 „   =   400   „
9 screw corvettes, of 20 guns, &c.

The active screw flotilla, consequently, possesses an armament of 1989 guns. If we add to this the armament of 80 paddle-wheel steamers, with 424 guns, we have a total for the steam fleet of 2404 guns—a power far superior to that of the steam fleets and flotillas in the whole world! We will close our account of the BRITISH NAVY,

by giving a list of the English fleets stationed in the
Baltic and Mediterranean during 1854 :—

THE BALTIC FLEET.

Sailing Vessels.

6 ships of the line, with 574 guns.
1 frigate, 42 ,,
1 corvette (hospital ship), 24 ,,
1 transport, — ,,
___

9 vessels. 640 guns.

Steamers.

Screw.	15 ships of the line,	1229 guns,	6960 horse-power.
	3 frigates,	111 ,,	960 ,,
	4 corvettes,	58 ,,	762 ,,
	2 transports,	16 ,,	800 ,,
Paddle-wheel.	5	62 ,,	2740 ,,
	3	38 ,,	1200 ,,
	1	6 ,,	320 ,,
	3	18 ,,	800 ,,
	8	19 ,,	888 ,,

Total, 44 steamers, 1557 gns. 15,430 horse-power.

Total strength of the Baltic fleet (1854) :—52 vessels, with 2197 guns, and 15,430 horse-power.

THE MEDITERRANEAN FLEET (BLACK SEA).

Sailing Vessels.

8 ships of the line, = 778 guns.
2 frigates, = 100 ,,
2 corvettes, = 45 ,,
2 transports, = 10 ,,
___

11 ships, = 943 guns.

Steamers.

Screw	{	2 ships of the line of	161	guns and	950	horse-power.
	{	3 corvettes,	49	„	750	„
	⌈	1	21	„	800	„
		2	28	. „	1875	„
Paddle	⎨	4	56	„	1677	„
wheel		4	16	„	1398	„
		6	27	„	1400	„
		1	8	„	160	„
	⌊	1	8	„	40	„

Total,   24 steamers.   371 guns.   8250 horse-power.

Total strength of the Mediterranean fleet (1854) :—
38 vessels, with 1,314 guns, and 8,250 horse-power.

As a reserve, there are in English ports at least 14
ships of the line (sail and screw), 4 frigates (do.), and
a number of smaller vessels, altogether about 48 vessels, with 1768 guns, and 9880 horse-power.

INDIAN NAVY.

> 1 commodore as commandant.
> 8 captains.
> 16 commanders.
> 68 lieutenants.
> 13 mates.
> 73 midshipmen.
> 14 paymasters.
> 12 captain's clerks.

The number of vessels belonging to the Company
was—

1 ship of 20 guns.
2 ships of 16 „
4 brigs with 21 guns.
2 schooners 6 „
2 cutters 4 „
2 gunboats 8 „
And 23 steamers 89 „

The Presidency of Bengal has also a special pilot corps of 17 steamers, with 11 guns, and about 16 other pilot vessels.

II.

THE FRENCH ARMY AND NAVY.

THE FRENCH ARMY.

THE affairs of the French army are administered by the Ministry of War, — divided into 7 principal branches, at the head of each of them being a general.

1st direction (personal affairs) containing 7 bureaux.
2d   ,,   (artillery)   ,,   2 sections.
3d   ,,   (engineers)   ,,   2   ,,
4th   ,,   (administration)   ,,   5 bureaux.
5th   ,,   (Algeria)   ,,   4   ,,
6th   ,,   (war depôt)   ,,   2   ,,
7th   ,,   (accounts)   ,,   6   ,,

To the Ministry of War are also attached the following consulting committees, composed of generals and staff officers :—

Committee of the general staff.
        ,,   infantry.
        ,,   cavalry.
        ,,   artillery.
        ,,   fortifications.
        ,,   surgery, &c.
Veterinary commission.
Commission of public works.

The general staff is divided into the staff of the army and the corps of the general staff (état major).

STAFF OF THE ARMY.

6 marshals. 80 generals of division. 160 ,, brigade.	Active, or 1st section.
71 generals of division. 173 ,, brigade.	Reserve, or 2d section.
52 generals of division. 70 ,, brigade.	Pensioned.

Generals of brigade, after passing their 62d year, and generals of division, at the age of 65, are attached to the reserve, with two-thirds of their former pay, but are liable to be called upon to serve in case of war.

THE CORPS OF THE GENERAL STAFF.

This contains, including adjutants—

30 colonels.
30 lieutenant-colonels.
100 chefs d'escadron.
300 captains.
100 lieutenants.

———

560 officers.

From this corps all the adjutancies of the army, as well as the whole of the general staffs of the military divisions and subdivisions, are derived. Another portion is employed in the war ministry as war depôt, comprising the topographical, historical, and other branches; and one captain of the second class is selected from this corps, for service with each infantry and cavalry regiment.

The whole of France has been recently formed into
21 military divisions,* and 3 in Algeria. These 24
divisions are again subdivided into 86 subdivisions,
agreeing with the number of departments. The first
are commanded by generals of division, the latter by
generals of brigade. Each division has a general staff. All the troops
for home military establishments, &c., in the various
districts, are under the special jurisdiction of the commanders of the division. The special officers, as the
staffs of the strong places, and the administration
officers, are also under his authority.

The general staff of the fortresses.	154 town commandants. 12 town majors. 138 adjutants. 24 secretaries of division.
General staff of the artillery.	23 brigade and division generals. 136 staff officers. 342 captains. 17 lieutenants.
General staff of the engineers.	14 generals of division and brigade. 151 staff officers. 309 captains. 3 lieutenants.

The administration contains 670 officers for all
branches (clothing and lodging of troops, hospitals,
&c.)†

* The French army is not divided into corps d'armée divisions : the
only exception is the recently formed guard in imitation of the old Imperial Guard. This consists of 2 infantry brigades of 2 regiments of
grenadiers, each of 3 battalions ; 2 regiments of voltigeurs, each also of
3 battalions ; 1 cavalry brigade of 1 regiment cuirassiers and 1 of guides,
each of 6 squadrons ; 2 battalions of gendarmerie of the guard ; 5 horse
batteries, with depôt ; and 1 company of engineers.
† These statistics refer equally to Algeria.

The army is composed of THE ACTIVE TROOPS, and TROOPS FOR HOME SERVICE.

1. ACTIVE TROOPS.

(1.) *Infantry.*

75 regiments of line infantry.
25   „   light infantry.
30 battalions chasseurs au pied.
 3 regiments Zuaves.
 2   „   foreign legion.
 3 battalions light African infantry.
 3   „   native infantry.
12 disciplinary companies.
Total—105 regiments ; 26 battalions.

Each line or light infantry regiment is composed of 3 battalions, and one depôt battalion of 8 companies, of which 1 company are grenadiers (rifles in the light infantry), 6 companies fusiliers, and 1 company voltigeurs.

A regiment is made up as follows :—

1 colonel.
1 lieutenant-colonel.
1 major.
3 captains, adjutants-majors.
1 lieutenant (ensign).
1 lieutenant of the general staff.
1 captain (paymaster).
1 lieutenant (deputy paymaster).
1 captain (uniform, &c.).
3 surgeons.
1 ensign.

20 non-commissioned officers and sappers.
52 musicians.
3 battalions, including their depôt companies :
Or, altogether, amounting to 3351 men.

The African line battalions contain one company
less; and, consequently, the regiments, with depôt,
only 2510 men.

The line infantry are armed with percussion guns
and bayonet; light regiments and voltigeur companies carry short rifles; sappers and bandsmen are
armed with a short carbine and bayonet.

1 battalion of chasseurs au pied contains 10 companies, made up of 1 major, 1 lieutenant, and 1 sub-
lieutenant; 105 bandsmen, and rank and file ; or, at
the full strength, 122 men.

A battalion is thus made up :—

    1 chef de bataillon
    1 captain, performing duties of major.
    1 captain, aide-major.
    1 lieutenant (firing inspector).
    1 lieutenant (paymaster).
    1 officer (for uniforms, &c.)
    1 surgeon.
    10 companies.

Or, altogether, amounting to 1288 men.

The chasseurs are armed with rifles (carabine à tige)
and sword-bayonet.

The strength of the home infantry will, consequently, amount to 100 regiments of line and light
infantry, 20 battalions of chasseurs au pied = about
360,000 men.

1 regiment of Zuaves = 3 battalions of 9 companies, including 1 depôt = 9330 men.

1 regiment of the foreign legion = 3 battalions of 8 companies (including 2 élite) = 3050 men.

1 battalion of light African infantry = 3 battalions of 10 companies (including 2 depôts and 1 élite) = 1240 men.

1 battalion of native infantry of 8 companies = 1000 men.

The strength of the African infantry will, consequently, amount to about 22,000 men, divided into 21 battalions, and the total strength of the French infantry to

341 BATTALIONS, or 382,000 MEN.

(2.) Cavalry.

12 regiments of reserve cavalry (2 carbineers, 10 cuirassiers).
20   „   line   „   (12 dragoons, 8 lancers).
29   „   light   „   (12 chasseurs à cheval).
 9 hussars, 4 African chasseurs, 3 spahis, 1 guides, of the general staff.

Each cavalry regiment is composed of 6 squadrons (exclusive of 1 depôt).

A squadron of reserve cavalry is made up of—

1 captain, commanding.
1 second captain.
1 upper lieutenant.
1 lieutenant.
4 under lieutenants.
27 non-commissioned officers.
4 trumpeters.
139 horsemen.

Or, 178 combatants, 3 non-effectives, and 173 horses.

A regiment of reserve cavalry is composed of—

1 colonel.
1 lieutenant-colonel.
3 chefs d'escadron.
1 captain (instructor).
3 captains (adjutants-majors).
1 lieutenant (standard-bearer).
1 lieutenant (general staff).
4 officers (administration, &c.).
4 surgeons.
7 non-commissioned officers and trumpeters.
57 secretaries, workmen, &c.
6 squadrons and depôts.

Together amounting, on a war footing, to 1357 men, 1282 horses.

1 squadron of line cavalry = 188 combatants, 3 non-combatants, 183 horses.

1 regiment of line cavalry, with depot = 1421 men, 1352 horses.

1 squadron of light cavalry = 198 combatants, 3 non-combatants, 193 horses.

1 regiment of light cavalry, with depot = 1491 men, 1422 horses.

(The officers are the same as in reserve regiments.)

1 regiment of guides = 1636 men, 1545 horses.

The strength of the French cavalry, therefore, amounts to 54 regiments of about 78,000 men, with 74,000 horses.

1 regiment of African chasseurs generally contains 857 men and 810 horses.

1 regiment of spahis—1187 men, 1224 horses (these troops carry long rifles, slung on shoulder).

The strength of the African cavalry will be 7 regiments = 8700 men, with 8500 horses.

	Regiments.	Men.	Horses.
French cavalry	54	78,000	74,000
African ,,	7	8,700	8,500

The total strength of the French cavalry of all arms will consequently amount to about 86,000 men, with 82,000 horses.

(3.) *Artillery.*

According to the organisation introduced on the 14th February 1854, by which the artillery train, hitherto separate, was incorporated with the batteries, the artillery is composed of the following divisions :—

1. General staff of the artillery—8 generals of division and 16 of brigade.

2. Special general staff of the artillery, made up of—

> 31 colonels.
> 33 lieutenant-colonels.
> 41 chefs d'escadron (majors).
> 115 captains, 1st class.
> 15 captains, 2d class.
> 80 captains (attached to the fortress).

Further—

833 military officers (inspectors of laboratories and fortresses, &c.).

117 civil officers (comptrollers, managers of foundries and gunshops, &c.).

3. The artillery troops :—

5 regiments of foot for fortress artillery = 60 batteries.
1   „   artillery pontonniers   =   12 companies.
7   „   line artillery   = 105 batteries.
4   „   horse artillery   =   32   „
—   ———
17 regiments, or   197 batteries.

To these must be added 12 laboratory companies, 1 company of manufacturers of arms (to be raised to 5).

1 regiment foot artillery is made up of the staff, rank and file, 12 foot batteries, 6 park batteries, 1 depôt.

1 regiment of artillery pontonniers—staff, non-commissioned officers, 12 companies of pontonniers, 4 companies of drivers, 1 depôt.

1 regiment of horse artillery is made up of the staff, non-commissioned officers, 8 mounted batteries, and 1 depôt.

The French artillery are armed with carbines.

A horse battery — 4 officers, 30 non-commissioned officers, 189 gunners and drivers = 226 combatants, 268 horses, 26 vehicles.

A flying battery = 4 officers, 30 non-commissioned officers, 3 trumpeters, 179 gunners and drivers = 216 combatants, 214 horses, 30 vehicles.

A foot battery—4 officers, 28 non-commissioned officers, 2 buglers, 166 gunners and drivers = 200 combatants, 10 horses.

The officers are—1 captain commanding, 1 second captain, 1 upper lieutenant, 1 lieutenant or sub-lieutenant.

STAFF OF AN ARTILLERY REGIMENT.

1 colonel.
1 lieutenant-colonel.
1 major.
1 captain (riding master).
2 captains (adjutants-majors).
3 captains and lieutenants (administration).
1 lieutenant of general staff.
4 surgeons.
57 non-commissioned officers and artizans.

Or, 18 combatants, 62 non-combatants, 50 horses.

The 12 laboratory companies and the gunmakers' company together have a strength of 1452 men.

The total strength of the French artillery, without depôt and pontonniers, is—197 batteries, with about 157,000 men, 49,000 horses, and 1182 guns.

A company of pontonniers is composed of—

4 officers (same as in artillery).
26 non-commissioned officers.
2 buglers.
102 pontonniers.
_____
134 combatants, 19 horses.

The regiment is made up of—

1 colonel.
1 lieutenant-colonel.
4 chefs de bataillon.
2 majors.
2 adjutants-majors.

2 captains } (administration.)
1 lieutenant
3 surgeons.
33 non-commissioned officers, artizans, &c.
12 companies.
4 train companies.

Or, 1920 men ; 642 horses.

ENGINEERS.

3 regiments of engineers.
2 laboratory companies of engineers.

1 regiment. { 2 battalions of 8 companies (7 sappers, 1 miners) ; 1 company train.

1 sapper { 2 captains (1st and 2d), 1 first-lieutenant, 1 lieutenant, 22 non-commissioned officers and workmen, 2 drummers, and 124 men.
and miner
company.

1 train company = 4 officers, 18 non-commissioned officers, 2 buglers, 100 men = 124 men, with 210 horses.

A regiment of engineers is made up of—

1 colonel.
1 lieutenant-colonel.
2 chefs de bataillon.
1 major.
1 captain aide-major.
1 lieutenant (ensign).
2 captains } (administration, &c.)
1 lieutenant
3 surgeons.

D

100 non-commissioned officers, &c.

17 companies.

Or, 2533 combatants, 74 non-combatants, and 210 horses.

2 companies of engineer workmen = 400 men.

The engineers are armed in a similar manner to the light infantry.

Strength of the engineer corps = 8221 men; 630 horses.

TROOPS FOR THE SERVICE OF THE ADMINISTRATION.

1 battalion of workmen = 6 companies (without 1 depôt) attached to the lazarettos, &c. = 1780 men.

1 corps of military transport. { 5 parks, with 644 men.
5 squadrons transport = 35 companies (exclusive of 5 depôt) = 6895 men.

Total strength of this branch :—5 parks, 50 companies, and 9300 men.

SANITARY CORPS.

This is made up of—

5 inspectaires.
48 principaux.
66 ordinaires.
285 majors.
45 adjoints.
468 aïde-majors.
460 sous-aides.

Or, 1377 men, all of officers' rank.

THE MILITARY SCHOOLS.

1. The polytechnic school at Paris. ⎫ Preparatory schools
2. The special school at St Cyr.   ⎬ for officers.
3. The military college at La Fléche. ⎭

4. The firing school at Vincennes.   ⎫
5. The pyrotechnic school at Metz.   ⎪ Special schools.
6. The military medical school at Paris. ⎬
7. The veterinary school at Alfortze.   ⎭

8. The school of the general staff at Paris.   ⎫ Exercising
9. The engineer and artillery school at Metz.   ⎬ schools.
10. The cavalry school at Saumur.   ⎭

In addition to these, we find regimental schools for under officers of the cavalry and the line; firing schools for officers and non-commissioned officers, for infantry regiments, and chasseur battalions; 12 artillery and 3 engineer schools for non-commissioned officers and soldiers.

RE-MOUNTS AND VETERINARY SURGEONS.

There are in France 7 re-mount depôts and 18 succursals—the former presided over by staff-officers, the latter by captains of cavalry and artillery. The veterinary surgeons' *cadre* is as follows :—

	⎧ Principaux	. .	6 ⎫	
Veterinaires.	⎨ En premier	. .	102 ⎬	270 men.
	⎪ Aides	. . .	124 ⎨	
	⎩ Sous-aides	. .	38 ⎭	

TROOPS FOR HOME SERVICE.

Gendarmerie, Veterans, and National Guard.

GENDARMERIE :—26 legions in the departments; 1 legion in Algiers; together, 94 companies. 20

companies of colonial and élite gendarmerie; 16
companies and 4 squadrons garde de Paris; 5 companies sapper-pompiers. Altogether, 25,400 men,
among whom there are 802 officers and 14,000
mounted men.

The gendarmerie is only made up from the active
army, and is, consequently, calculated to form part
of it.

VETERANS:—18 companies of 1794 men. They
are partly invalids.

NATIONAL GUARDS:—The strength of these is un-
decided, and rests with the Government; but all
Frenchmen of good body, between 25 and 50, are
bound to serve in it. They are generally only employed to maintain internal order; and only in case
of need are they called upon to join the active army.
Since the *coup d'état*, their number has been considerably lessened; and there is no idea of employing
them in the field. At the same time, the present Government, who justly feared them, and only formally
respected them as a historical tradition, have retained the privilege of nominating the higher officers.
Nevertheless, the National Guard form an important
factor in the armament of France; for they might
easily be raised to a strength of 300 battalions of
1000 men.

The National Guard are generally under the civil
authorities, and only during war under the military.
The State provides their armament; all the rest is
left to the communes. Without the special permission
of the Minister of the Interior, they only form infantry corps, subdivided into companies, battalions,

and legions—each battalion consisting of from 4 to 8 companies. In Paris, however, we find cavalry.

From these data, we find that the total strength of the French army would amount to about 566,000 men, with 82,000 horses and 1182 guns; to which must be added, 180,000 soldiers, dismissed after seven years' service, or recruits not yet called in; as well as 100,000 National Guards; or, altogether, 280,000 men more. Of these, 80,000 were hitherto stationed in Africa.

REMARKS.—General conscription, between the ages of 20 and 27, with substitution; and it may be generally assumed, that the soldier serves for four to five years. Those soldiers dismissed after seven years' service, form, with the fourth portion of the recruits not called out, the reserve, or the second battalion. The National Guard form the third battalion. During peace, one-third of the sub-lieutenants are drawn from the non-commissioned officers; two-thirds from the military schools. The higher charges, inclusive of the major, are selected, half by choice, half by seniority. The military regulations of France are generally very good. The troops are well equipped and dressed. The cavalry, however, have always been inferior to the other arms, as, upon investigation, at least 12,000 horses must be obtained from other countries.

THE FRENCH NAVY.

MINISTRY OF THE MARINE.

General staff—1 admiral, 1 captain, and 2 lieutenants.

Council of the Admiralty. { 4 admirals, 2 captains, 1 director of marine building, 1 engineer do., 1 commissary-general, and 1 comptroller.

The Council of the Admiralty is attached to the Ministry of Marine, which contains several subdivisions—

1. The cabinet of the Minister.
2. Four directions (personal, *matériel*, colonies, and accounts).
3. The division of invalids.
4. The general controls.
5. Five general inspections (docks and harbours, medical, ordnance, *matériel*, and marines).

To the Ministry of Marine are also attached—

1. The Marine Council. { 5 admirals, 2 captains, 5 engineers, 2 inspectors-general of docks and ordnance *matériel*.
2. The commission for the improvement of the naval school and invalids.
3. The general depôt of maps and charts.

France possesses large factories and ateliers for the marine artillery; and foundries (the latter capable of turning out 900 guns *per annum*), numerous arsenals, and establishments for maritime instruction.

THE FLEET.

Naval Officers.

Admirals . . .	2	(in war, 3.)
Vice-do.	10	
Rear-do.	20	
Captains of ships of the line	100	
Captains of frigates . .	230	
Lieutenants of ships of the line	650	
Ensigns	600	
Aspirants of the first class	200	

Total, 1812

To these must be added the reserve *cadres*—7 vice-admirals, 12 rear-admirals, 100 to 120 aspirants of the second class, and volunteers of the first and second class.

PETTY OFFICERS, MEN, &c.

Engineers	144	men.
Surgeons, apothecaries, &c. . .	561	„
Chaplains	13	„
Purveyors and other clerks . .	1,011	„
Harbour gendarmerie . . .	298	„ (17 officers.)
Artillery, in 23 artillery, and 6 artizan corps ; with 1 general, 25 staff, 162 officers, and 3295 men . .	3,483	„
Marines, with 3 regiments of 4 companies ; with 1 general, 48 staff, 443 officers, and 11,859 men .	12,351	„
Corps of petty officers . . .	1,760	„

Sailors, &c., in 5 divisions, of 180 companies ; 7 depôt companies, of about 103 men. In addition, 2 companies of gunners, 4 companies of ships' boys, 2 companies of stokers.

These contingents are provided by the marine inscription (existing since 1683), which comprises all the seamen of France up to their 50th year. In 1853, these lists furnished an amount of 152,565 men, and as only 96,000 men, calculating from the captain downwards, are required to man the fleet of 328 vessels, it will be seen that France is abundantly provided with sailors.

CREWS OF FRENCH SHIPS OF WAR.

Sailing Ships.	Ships of the line, according to rank,	677	to	1087	men.
	Frigates,	„	„	326 „	513	„
	Corvettes,	„	„	110 „	228	„
	Brigs,	„	„	92 „	113	„
	Light ships,	„	„	61 „	74	„
	Transports,	„	„	45 „	154	„
Stmrs.	Ships of the line,	„	„	500 „	600	„
	Frigates,	„	„	350 „	400	„
	Corvettes,	„	„	120 „	180	„
	Avisos,	„	„	43 „	80	„

These crews are divided in the larger vessels as follows :—

	SHIPS OF THE LINE. 1st Class	FRIGATES. 1st Class.	CORVETTES. 1st Class.
Officers ⎫	15	9	6
Aspirants ⎬ great staff.....	13	8	4
Surgeons ⎪	5	4	2
Clerks ⎭	1	1	1
Small staff......................	8	8	7
Petty officers.................	89	43	22
Fouriers........................	7	4	2
Sailors (inscription).........	721	307	122
Do. (conscription)	169	91	39
Boys	39	21	12
Storekeepers, &c.............	50	17	11
Total,	1117	513	228

STATE OF THE FLEET.

Before the commencement of the present war, the French fleet, in active service, contained 12 to 15 ships of the line, 30 to 36 frigates, 30 to 36 corvettes, 60 to 65 light, and 20 to 25 transport ships; altogether, 150 to 160 vessels, with a strength of 30,000 to 35,000 men.

At the commencement of 1854, however, France had the following ships at her disposition:—

Ships of the Line.

Sailing Vessels.		Screws.		
1st class,	7	.	2, 790 h.-power.	
2d „	7	.	7, 4440 „	53, with 5,096 guns.
3d „	15	.	4, 2220 „	
4th „	11	.		

Frigates.

1st „	} 42	.		58, with 3955 „
2d „				
3d „	15	.	1, 220 „	

Corvettes.

37	.	2, 240 „	39, with 868 „

Light Ships.

100	.	1, 30 „	101, with 1066 „

Transport Ships.

39		788 „

Total, 290 vessels, with 11,773 guns; 17, with 7920 horse-power, being screws.

Steamers.

Ships of the line . . 7 ⎤
Frigates . . . . 20 ⎪
Corvettes . . . . 30 ⎬ With 32,350 horse-power.
Avisos . . . . 64 ⎪
——— ⎪
Total, 121 ⎦

The steamers are principally armed with Paixhans and long 30-pounder guns.

In 1854, France had 5 different squadrons at sea, as follows :—

	Ships of Line.	Frigates.	Corvts.	Trnspts.	Total.	Guns.
1. Baltic	9 .	10 .	3 .	9 .	31 .	1266
2. Black Sea 15	.	8 .	3 .	3 .	29 .	1610
3. Grecian Archipelago 0	.	2 .	3 .	9 .	14 .	146
4. Transport division ⎱ at Toulon......... ⎰	0	. 9	. 8	. 0	. 17	. 0
5. Reserve 14	.	0 .	0 .	0 .	14 .	1390
	38	29	17	21	105	4412

Of these vessels, 53 were propelled by steam.

III.

THE RUSSIAN ARMY AND NAVY.

THE RUSSIAN ARMY.

GENERAL STAFF OF THE EMPEROR.

This is composed, at the present moment, of—

1 War Minister.
1 quartermaster-general.
1 general master of the ordnance.
1 inspector-general of engineering.
1 inspector   do.
1 inspector-general of artillery.
1   „   „   cavalry.
1 dufour general.
1 commandant of the imperial head-quarters.
1 supreme inspector of medicine.
1 general of the carriage department.
1 master of the stables.
1 chaplain-general.

ADJUTANT GENERALS.

The Grand Duke Constantine.
1 general field-marshal.
1 general of engineers.

6 generals of artillery.
12   „   infantry.
11   „   cavalry.
1 admiral.
30 lieutenant-generals.
4 vice-admirals.
4 major-generals.

ATTACHED TO THE EMPEROR'S SUITE.

The Grand Dukes Nicholas and Michael.
37 major-generals.
2 rear-admirals.

WING ADJUTANTS.

27 colonels.
3 lieutenant-colonels.
1 major.
5 captains (including 1 of the navy).
3 captain-lieutenants.
7 captains of cavalry (naval).
1 staff-captain.
4 staff-captains (cavalry).
1 cornet.

ATTACHES TO THE EMPEROR.

3 generals of infantry.
1 general of cavalry.

THE MINISTRY OF WAR

Contains the following departments :—

1. The council of war for military jurisdiction and administration, formed of 10 generals.

2. The chancellerie of the War Minister, in 4 divisions, for justice, archives, registration, and military proclamations, (1 major-general as director, with 14 officers as clerks).

3. The auditor's department of 3 generals of infantry and 5 lieutenant-generals.

4. The departments as follows:—

> (1.) The topographical bureau (1 lieutenant-general).
>
> (2.) The inspection (1 general, 2 colonels, and 9 officers of lower grade).
>
> (3.) The artillery affairs (1 lieutenant-general and 8 clerks).
>
> (4.) The engineers (1 lieutenant-general and 5 clerks).
>
> (5.) The administration (1 commissary-general of war, 1 lieutenant-general, and 8 clerks).
>
> (6.) The commissariat (1 commissary-general, 1 major-general, and 7 clerks).
>
> (7.) The military colonies (1 lieutenant-general, 3 vice-directors, 3 councillors, 3 colonels of Cossacks, 2 state-councillors, and 6 officers of special arms).
>
> (8.) The medical affairs (1 privy councillor).
>
> (9.) Administration of justice (1 auditor-general).

5. The imperial chancellerie of war (2 clerks).

6. The chancery of imperial head-quarters (1 master-general and 1 captain).

7. The committees of the War Ministry:—

(1.) The committee of inspection (1 general of infantry and 25 members).

(2.) The military censorship (1 lieutenant-general and 9 members).

(3.) The military medical committee (1 inspector-general and 24 members).

(4. and 5.) The committees of infantry and cavalry (president and 12 generals each).

(6.) The committee of invalids (president and 1 general).

(7.) The committee for ecclesiastical affairs.

(8.) The committee for the improvement of arms (president, 1 lieutenant-general, and 12 members).

(9.) The editor of the military journal, *The Invalid* (editor and 1 general).

The Ministry of War, the general staff of the Emperor, and the staff of the army, described below, are both in peace and war; in special cases, however, the staff of the active army and of the army corps are set in motion, their composition being analogous to that of the first portion of the imperial staff.

THE LAND FORCES.

The Russian land forces may be divided into five principal categories—the army-in-chief (active troops of the first year of service), the reserve, the garrison troops or internal guard battalions, and invalids, the gendarmerie, the irregular troops, and the model and instructing troops.

THE ACTIVE ARMY.

THE GENERAL STAFF.

The general staff, of which the Minister of War is chief, is divided into the actual general staff, and the topographical corps. The former, excepting the general staff of the guards, and the army, is subdivided into the great general staff, and the general staff of the troops.

The great general staff is composed of 45 generals, staff and subaltern officers, who are divided into their special departments. The general staff of the troops, whose chief is a general, is attached to each corps d'armée.

The topographical corps is divided into 6 sections —the topographical, astronomical, mechanical, section for printers and engravers, the chancellerie, and archives.

1. INFANTRY.

Russia possesses 12 guard, 8 grenadier, 4 carbineer, 42 line infantry, 42 chasseur, regiments; 1 battalion tirailleurs of the guard, 1 grenadier, 7 rifle, and a number of independent battalions, collectively divided into the guards and grenadiers. The 6 infantry corps, the special corps, the Caucasus, Finland, Siberia, and Orenburg, in which latter formation the suitable troops of other arms are attached to them.

E

(1.) THE GUARDS :—3 guard infantry divisions, 6 brigades, 12 regiments.

> 3 guard chasseur regiments, attached to the 2d, 4th, and 6th brigades.
> 1 sapper battalion to the 4th brigade.
> 1 Finland guard, rifle battalion, attached to 6th brigade.
> 1 train battalion.
> 1 regiment = 3 battalions (exclusive of 1 reserve, and 1 depôt battalion) = 12 companies = 67 officers, 136 musicians. 3000 combatants, 132 non-effectives.
> 1 company = 4 officers, 20 non-commissioned officers, 8 musicians, and 236 men.

(2.) THE GRENADIER CORPS :—3 divisions = 6 brigades = 12 regiments. 3 carbineer regiments, with the 2d, 4th, and 6th brigades.

> 1 grenadier sapper battalion attached to the 2d brigade.
> 1 grenadier rifle battalion.
> 1 reserve battalion.
> 1 reserve grenadier brigade (with the Caucasian corps).
> 1 train battalion.

Formation of the regiments, &c., like that of the guards. The carbineer regiments stand in the same relation to the grenadier regiments, as the chasseur regiments to the line infantry.

(3.) THE 6 INFANTRY CORPS, each 3 divisions =

6 brigades = 12 regiments (with each brigade, 1 chasseur regiment).

> 1 tirailleur battalion.
> 1 train battalion.
> Each line and chasseur regiment = 4 battalions (exclusive of 1 reserve, and 1 depôt battalion) = 16 companies = 89 officers, 155 musicians, 4008 combatants, and 182 non-effectives.
> A company = 4 officers, 20 non-commissioned officers, 8 musicians, and 230 men.

(4.) THE CAUCASIAN CORPS:—3 divisions = 6 brigades = 12 regiments (with each division, 1 chasseur regiment).

> 1 Caucasian tirailleur battalion.
> 1 reserve grenadier brigade = 2 regiments (1 of them carbineers), with half a train battalion.
> 18 Georgian line battalions, in 3 brigades.
> 16 line battalions of the Black Sea, in 3 divisions.
> 13 Caucasian line battalions, in 2 brigades.
> An infantry or chasseur regiment = 4 battalions (excluding 2 reserve battalions) = 111 officers, 183 musicians, 5650 combatants, 296 non-effectives, 283 invalids.
> A line battalion = 18 officers, 18 musicians, 1002 combatants, and 35 non-effectives.

(5.) THE FINLAND CORPS:—1 division = 2 brigades = 12 battalions = 12,600 men.

> A battalion = 20 officers, 18 musicians, 1002 combatants, 32 non-effectives.

(6.) THE SIBERIAN CORPS:—1 division = 3 brigades = 15 battalions (excluding 3 garrison battalions) = 15,800 men.

A battalion = 27 officers, 18 musicians, 1002 combatants, 22 to 47 non-effectives.

(7.) THE ORENBURG CORPS:—1 division = 2 brigades = 10 battalions = 10,500 men.

A battalion = 21 officers, 18 musicians, 1002 combatants, 22 to 46 non-effectives.

Hence the total strength of the infantry (without reserve and depôt battalions) = 507 battalions, with about 540,000 effectives. The line and light infantry are armed with percussion guns and bayonets; the rifles with Deloigne rifles and couteaux de chasse. There is, however, only an external distinction between the light and line infantry, as their manœuvres are generally the same. The tirailleurs form the only actual light infantry Russia possesses.

2. CAVALRY.

The regular Russian cavalry, of 12 heavy (cuirassier), 38 light (20 lancers, 16 hussars, 2 Cossack), and 11 dragoon regiments. 1 guard cavalry corps, 7 light cavalry divisions of the grenadier and infantry corps, and 2 reserve cavalry corps.

(1.) THE GUARD CAVALRY CORPS:—

3 Divisions.
{ 1 division cuirassiers = 2 brigades = 4 regiments.
2 divisions light cavalry = 4 brigades = 8 regiments.
1 train battalion.

To the last divisions is also attached the Imperial Guard of Honour, composed of Tartars, Lesghis, Cossacks, &c.

(2.) LIGHT CAVALRY OF THE GRENADIER AND 6 ARMY CORPS :—

> To each of these corps are attached—1 light division = 2 brigades (1 lancer, 1 hussar) = 4 regiments.
> 1 train battalion.

(3.) THE RESERVE CAVALRY CORPS :—

1st Corps : 3 divisions.
{
1 division = 3 lancer, hussar, and dragoon brigades = 6 regiments.
2 divisions cuirassiers = 4 brigades = 8 regiments.
1 train battalion.
}

2d Corps : 3 divisions.
{
1 reserve lancer division = 2 brigades = 4 regiments.
2 divisions of dragoons = 4 brigades = 8 regiments.
(The 9th dragoon regiment is in the Caucasus).
1 train battalion.
}

Each cuirassier, guard hussar, guard lancer, guard dragoon, and guard Cossack regiment, contains 6 squadrons, in 3 divisions; each lancer and hussar regiment, 8 squadrons, in 4 divisions; each dragoon regiment, 10 squadrons; without taking into account, 1 reserve and 1 depôt squadron attached to each of these regiments.

> 1 guard cavalry regiment = 54 officers, 22 musicians, 1006 combatants, and 101 non-effectives.
> 1 squadron = 8 officers, 3 musicians, 191 combatants, and 15 non-effectives.
> 1 lancer or hussar regiment of the grenadier and

6 corps d'armée = 64 officers, 25 musicians, 1433 combatants, and 111 non-effectives.

1 cuirassier or lancer regiment of the reserve = 54 officers, 39 musicians, 1092 combatants, and 109 non-effectives.

1 dragoon regiment of the reserve = 77 officers, 39 musicians, 1790 combatants, and 123 non-effectives.

Total strength of the cavalry—466 squadrons, with about 80,000 men.

The arms of the cavalry are percussioned.

3. ARTILLERY.

Russia has heavy and light foot and horse batteries, which all contain 8 guns, up to those stationed in the Caucasus, and mountain batteries.

1 heavy foot battery.	4	12-pounder guns.		7 officers, 258 men, 152 horses.
	4	20	„	howitzers.	
1 heavy horse battery.	8	20	„	„	8 officers, 286 men, 378 horses.
A light foot battery.	16	6	„	guns.	7 officers, 203 men, 131 horses.
	2	20	„	howitzers.	
A horse battery.	4	6	„	guns.	7 officers, 221 men, 287 horses.
	4	10	„	howitzers.	
A mountain battery.	10	10	„	„	320 men.
	4	10	„	mortars.	
A heavy battery in the Caucasus.	6	6	„	guns.	...
	6	10	„	howitzers.	
A light battery in the Caucasus.	4	6	„	guns.	...
	4	10	„	howitzers.	

The whole artillery forms 9 foot and 2 horse divisions, which are attached to the various corps, in such a manner that each contains one.

1. The guard artillery division = 4 brigades.
{ 1st, 2d, 3d brigades, each of 2 heavy and 1 light battery.
1 horse brigade, of 3 light batteries.
Reserve—1 heavy horse battery.
1 light battery—Cossacks of the Don.
1 rocket battery. }

2. The grenadier artillery division = 4 brigades.
{ 1st, 2d, and 3d brigades, of 2 heavy and 2 light batteries.
1 horse brigade, of 2 light batteries. }

3. Each of the 6 artillery divisions of the infantry corps = 4 brigades.
{ 1 brigade = 2 heavy, 2 light batteries.
2d and 3d brigade = 1 heavy, 3 light batteries.
1 horse brigade = 2 light batteries. }

4. Each of 2 artillery divisions of the reserve cavalry corps.
{ 2 heavy, 4 light batteries. }

5. The Caucasian artillery division = 4 brigades.
{ 1 grenadier artillery brigade = 1 heavy, 1 light and 2 mountain batteries.
2 brigades, of 1 heavy, 2 light, and 1 mountain battery.
1 brigade, of 1 heavy, 1 light, and 2 mountain batteries.
1 moveable ammunition park. }

In addition, each artillery division has in the field 1 moveable reserve park.

The total strength of the Russian artillery, on the war footing, will amount to 162 foot and 30 horse batteries; with about 1400 guns and 44,000 men.

4. ENGINEER TROOPS.

The actual engineer corps contains, in addition to the engineer staff, the sappers and horse pioneer divisions.

Sapper Battalions.

The 9 sapper battalions for the several corps d'armée (exclusive of reserve cavalry) form 1 guard, 1 grenadier sapper brigade, 2 line sapper brigades, of 3 battalions, and 1 sapper brigade of the Caucasus. There are also 8 pontoon parks.

In the guard and grenadier battalions there are 2 miner companies.

In the line battalions there are 1 sapper and 3 pioneer companies.

In the Caucasian battalions, 2 sapper and 2 pioneer companies, each battalion having 1 train section attached to it.

Each pontoon park is formed of 1 pontoon company, with 12 pontoons. 1 sapper, miner, or pioneer company, has a strength of 4 officers, 256 non-commissioned officers and men. The armament, &c. of the sappers resembles that of the infantry.

There are 2 horse pioneer divisions, of 4 squadrons, attached to the guard and dragoon corps, each carrying 8 leathern pontoons.

Strength of the division, without the train section = 378 combatants, with a park of 24 vehicles, and 388 horses.

Strength of the mounted pioneer division = 731 men, with 64 pontoons.

Sappers and mounted pioneers, about 12,000 men.

Hence, the active army is thus composed :—

1. Corps of guards.
- 3 guard infantry divisions = 12 regiments.
- 1 „ rifle battalion.
- 1 „ reserve cavalry corps = 12 regiments.
- 1 guard artillery division = 15 batteries.
- 1 horse pioneer division = 32 pontoons.
- 1 guard sapper battalion.
- 1 train battalion.

About 59,000 men, with 112 guns.

2. The grenadier corps.
- 3 grenadier infantry divisions = 12 regiments.
- 1 grenadier tirailleur battalion.
- 1 light cavalry division = 4 regiments.
- 1 grenadier artillery division = 14 batteries.
- 1 grenadier sapper battalion.
- 1 train brigade.

About 51,000 men, with 112 guns.

3. The six infantry corps, each :
- 3 infantry divisions = 12 regiments.
- 1 rifle battalion.
- 1 light cavalry division = 4 regiments.
- 1 artillery division = 14 batteries.
- 1 sapper battalion.
- 1 pontoon park = 42 pontoons.
- 1 train brigade.

Each about 63,000 men, with 116 guns.

4. The two cavalry corps.

1.
- 2 cuirassier divisions = 8 regiments.
- 1 lancer division = 4 regiments.
- 1 horse artillery division = 6 batteries.
- 1 train brigade.

About 16,000 men, with 18 guns.

2.
- 2 dragoon divisions = 8 regiments.
- 8 horse artillery divisions, with a flying reserve park = 6 batteries.
- 1 horse pioneer division = 32 pontoons.
- 1 train brigade.

About 17,000 men, with 48 guns.

| 5. The Caucasian corps (exclusive of irregular troops). | 3 infantry divisions = 12 regiments.
1 tirailleur battalion.
47 line battalions.
1 reserve grenadier brigade = 2 regiments.
1 artillery division = 17 batteries.
1 dragoon regiment.
1 sapper battalion.
1 train brigade. | About 160,000 men, with 156 guns. |

Total strength of the Russian active army = 637,000 men, with 1436 guns, and 316 pontoons.*

RESERVES.

These troops are divided into the first and second reserves. To the former, those troops are attached for 5 years, who have been dismissed after 15 years' uninterrupted service ; to the other—the depôt battalions—all those troops which are disposable from that period till the expiration of their service—22 years in the guards, 25 in the line, and 20 in the military colonies. The first reserve is called out 3 weeks annually to exercise ; the second only by special command.

FIRST RESERVE.

Infantry. { Each infantry and chasseur regiment = 1 reserve battalion. To every 9 tirailleur battalions, 1 is attached as reserve. Strength equal to that of the active battalions.

---

* These troops would be the utmost Russia could bring together for the defence of her immense frontier, as the majority of the other troops can only be mobilised after some delay ; and it is well known that a portion of the troops above described generally only exists on paper. It would demand a very considerable time to concentrate the Russian reserves.

Cavalry. { With the exception of the grenadier cavalry regiments, each cavalry regiment of 6 or 8 squadrons = 1 reserve squadron, of 153 men. 1 dragoon regiment, of 10 squadrons = 2 reserve squadrons, of 153 men.

Artillery. { In the foot artillery, each brigade = 1 reserve battalion. In the horse artillery, each brigade of light guard, and 7 light cavalry divisions = 1 reserve battery. Each of the 6 horse reserve batteries of the infantry corps = one-half battery ; and each of the horse artillery division of the reserve cavalry = 1 battery.

Sappers. { Each sapper brigade = 1 reserve battalion, of the proper strength.

Mounted Pioneers. } Each division = one-half reserve squadron.

Caucasian corps. { Each infantry division = 1 reserve battalion, of the proper strength. Each dragoon brigade = 1 reserve squadron. 1 reserve sapper battalion.

First reserve = about 142,000 men, with 360 guns.

SECOND RESERVE.

Infantry. { Each infantry and chasseur regiment, exclusive of guard = 1 depôt battalion, of the same strength.

Cavalry. { Each cavalry regiment, exclusive of guards = 1 depôt squadron, of same strength.

Artillery. { With exception of horse and grenadier brigades, each brigade = 1 depôt battery, of the usual strength.

Sappers :—Each brigade = 1 depôt battalion, same strength.

Mounted Pioneers. { The division of the 2 reserve cavalry corps = one-half depôt squadron.

Caucasian corps. } 1 reserve division, of 5 battalions.

Second reserve = about 116,000 men, with 264 guns; or the two reserves, 258,000 men, with 624 guns.

GARRISON TROOPS, INVALIDS, GENS-DARMERIE.

The garrison troops principally perform the duties in the governmental towns, transporting recruits, &c., and are divided into infantry, artillery, and engineers. Their commandants are, at the same time, inspectors of the reserve companies.

Infantry. { 52 battalions, in 10 districts, of 4 companies; with about 28 officers, 17 musicians, 1000 effectives, 28 non-effectives (generally not reaching more than half this strength). The 15th, 16th, 19th, 20th, and 22d battalions have each 2 3-pounder howitzers.

Artillery. { 98 artillery companies, of 169 officers and men, in 12 districts, as fortress artillery, and serving the great park, of which the garrison artillery occupy the Caucasus and the forts there. It has at its disposal, 10 batteries, 7 arsenal companies, of the same strength as above, in the arsenals, foundries, &c.; 6 laboratory companies.

Engineers. { 10 generals, 340 officers, 25 military artizan companies, connected with 54 penal companies. } Attached to the various fortresses.

To these must be added—2 siege parks, of 240 waggons, 192 guns, as well as 2 engineer parks.

Strength of the garrison troops—about 78,000 men.

The invalids are divided into 818 companies, for orderly, courier, and other services.

The gensdarmerie, during peace, are attached to

the corps as military police, and amount, altogether, to $11\frac{1}{2}$ squadrons $= 2360$ men.

IRREGULAR TROOPS.

These consist principally of cavalry and horse artillery, with only very few infantry troops ; and are furnished by the Cossacks, Tartars, Calmucks, Caucasians, and other tribes. The cavalry is divided into brigades, of 2 to 3 regiments (polk), of 5 to 6 squadrons (sotnia) each, on an average, 150 men. The artillery has batteries of 4 6-pounder guns, and 4 10-pounder howitzers; or 6 6-pounder guns, and 6 10-pounder howitzers, whose strength varies, accordingly, from 200 to 300 men. The infantry is divided into sotnias of about 120 men, collected in weak battalions and regiments.

1. The army of the Cossacks of the Don.
- 56 regiments cavalry, of 6 sotnias, of 110 men, in 4 districts.
- 13 batteries, including 4 reserve batteries.
- 1 division in the arsenals.
- 1 sotnia military artizans.
- 5 sotnias frontier guardians and horse-catchers.
- * 2 regiments Cossacks of the guard, belonging to this army.

2. Cossacks of the Black Sea.
- 12 regiments cavalry, of 6 sotnias.
- 9 infantry battalions.
- 3 horse battalions.

3. The Caucasian Cossacks.
- 20 regiments, in 9 brigades.
- 3 horse batteries.

4. The Astrachan Cossacks.
- 3 regiments cavalry, of 6 sotnias.
- 1 horse battery.

5. The Orenburg Cossacks. { 10 regiments of cavalry, of 6 sotnias; 1 horse artillery brigade, of 3 batteries. 1 sotnia artificers and frontier officers.

6. The Ural Cossacks. } 12 regiments, of 5 sotnias.

7. The Bashkir and Metcheiasi Cossacks. } 17 regiments cavalry, of which the Bashkirs furnish 13.

8. The Siberian Cossacks of the line. { 4 brigades = 9 regiments of Cossacks of the line, of 6 sotnias. 3 horse batteries. 8 regiments infantry of Siberian urban Cossacks. 3 divisions of Siberian frontier Cossacks. 1 Tunger Cossack regiment. 4 regiments of schismatical Buriates.

9. Cossacks of the Azor. { 10 sotnias and 15 commandos, each of 20 men, in 29 vessels, cruising on the east coast of the Black Sea.

10. The Cossacks of the Danube. } 20 regiments, of 5 sotnias.

11. The Cossacks on Lake Beikal. } Recently formed; strength not known.

Total strength of the irregular troops, about 142,000 men, with 240 guns.

MODEL AND INSTRUCTING TROOPS.

Model troops. { 1 model infantry regiment. 1 „ cavalry „ 1 „ foot battery. 1 „ horse „ 1 „ battalion of the Caucasian corps.

Instructing troops. {
2 brigades, or 4 regiments of carbineers, of 5 battalions.
1 brigade, or 9 battalions artillery.
1 sapper battalion.
1 squadron cavalry.

CANTONIST DIVISIONS, AND SPECIAL SCHOOLS.

3 brigades = 9 battalions, 4 half-battalions, and 3 companies.
20 cavalry regiments.
5 horse batteries.
The schools of the guards, artillery division.
Sapper brigades and Cossacks.

In addition, we may mention the following educational establishments :—23 cadet and similar schools, 1 topographical, 1 engineer, 1 artillery, 1 ensigns of the guard, 1 general staff school (for officers), 11 garrison artillery schools, technical and surgical schools, schools for pyrotechnists and veterinary surgeons, &c.

MILITARY COLONIES.

After the termination of the war with France, in 1815, Alexander I. was induced to pay attention to every proposition which would support the troops in the cheapest manner. Count Araktchiyeff, who, by his talents alone, had been promoted to the rank of general of artillery, and who belonged to the war ministry, first proposed to quarter the soldiers on the crown serfs and build military villages according to a certain plan, giving each house a certain measure of land, and drew up a code of laws, by which these new colonies should be governed. The plan immediately received the imperial assent. Araktchiyeff intended by these colonies (1.) to avoid the expenses entailed by the maintenance of the army, and to cause the soldier partially to support himself by cultivating the land; (2.) to increase the reserve by the crown peasants, whose numbers would be equal to that of the colonised peasants ; (3.) the soldier would have a house, in which his family would find shelter, in case of war; and lastly (4.) to populate districts in a country where only a want of hands was perceptible, and convert many steppes into gardens and scattered towns.

Russian colonies were founded in the governments of Novgorod, Moghilev, Charkov, Kiev, Podolia, and Cherson, or in the vicinity of Poland, Austria, and Turkey. The choice of these localities was guided both by political and military views. The dominions of the Russian empire are vast; the troops levied in the north and east could but very slowly be moved to the southern provinces ; and, in case Russia desired to concentrate a larger portion of her troops in the vicinity of her southern and western provinces, this concentration would be remarkably assisted by having the numerous *personnel* of her military colonies on the frontiers.

The villages selected for the reception of the military colonies were all inhabited by crown peasants: they were freed from the imposts payable to the senate, and in lieu of them, were obliged to receive the soldiers intended to found the military colonies ; in the place of their cabins, houses were built in regular streets. These houses stood opposite to each other, and were separated by a yard. All the peasants, above 50 years of age, were selected to be appointed as master-colonists. Each master-colonist received 15 dessatmes of land (40 acres), for which he has to support a soldier and his family, and a horse in addition, if the village is occupied by a cavalry regiment; the soldier, in return, assists the colonist in cultivating his land, whenever military duties do not require a whole day. The soldier, who in this wise becomes a member of the family, receives the name of military peasant.

The officer is at liberty to select the soldiers to be quartered on the master-colonists: if the colonist have several sons, the eldest becomes his assistant; the second son belongs to the reserve; the third can become a military peasant; the others are incorporated as colonists or pupils. Thus, then, in founding these new arrangements, a fusion of two entirely different elements was attempted; so to speak, one class of the population was grafted on the other.

Numerous objections have been raised to the system introduced by Alexander I. But we believe that, in spite of its imperfections, it is the only one which can be easily carried into effect, and produce those remarkable results which are perceptible to all.

These agricultural soldiers, in fact, form the nucleus of the army in these colonies, and may be in time transfused to the whole empire. Their labour naturally depends upon the will of the officer. They can only till the land when exempt from military duties. The agricultural soldier always remains half peasant, half soldier, until he has served 25 years, if a Russian, 20 years if a Pole. After the expiration of this time, he is at liberty to leave the service. His place is filled up from the reserve. Near each master-

F

colonist's house is another exactly resembling it, occupied by the reserves, who may be regarded as the second self of the soldier. Each reserve man is selected by the colonel of the regiment from among the peasants, and is generally son or relation of the master-colonist. The reserve man is instructed in all the duties of a soldier, and in every respect so worked up, that he can immediately take the place of his principal. If the agricultural soldier dies, or falls in battle, the reserve man immediately takes his place. The reserve man is followed by the colonist, the latter by the boy. The master-colonist, the agricultural soldier, and the reserve man can choose their wives at their good pleasure. They are even encouraged to marry. On the other hand, the women belonging to a district dare not marry beyond its limits. The sons of master-colonists, agricultural soldiers, and reserve men, between the ages of 13 and 17, are called cantonists. They are exercised as soldiers, but they also attend school. The boys between 8 and 13 years of age attend the school of the village in which their parents live, and are exercised every other day. They and the cantonists are all dressed in uniform and counted as soldiers. All the children of the male sex are sent to schools, where they are taught reading, writing, and arithmetic, on the principle of mutual instruction. They learn here by heart a species of catechism of the duties of the soldier; they are taught the sword exercise and riding, and when they have attained their 14th year, they are assembled at head-quarters and collected into corps, when those who have distinguished themselves by talent and attention are appointed officers. The various components of a colonial village may, consequently, be regarded as follows :—

(1.) The master-colonist, the pater familias.

(2.) His assistant, who assists him in cultivating the land.

(3.) The agricultural soldier, who assists him when off duty.

(4.) The reserve man, who is substituted for the soldier in case of need.

(5.) The cantonists from 13 to 17 years of age.

(6.) The lads from 8 to 13.

(7.) Children of the male sex under 8 years of age.

(8.) The females.

(9.) The invalids.

The colonists of southern Russia occupy 380 villages in the Government of Cherson, Charkov, and Yekaterinoslav. The crown has here 30,000 crown peasants. Each village contains, according to its size, from two to three squadrons : there are, consequently, in these villages, 80,000 men. These military districts, or the portion of the country in which the military colonies are situate, are so stringently separated from the rest of the Government, that no person may enter them, without a special pass from the military authorities. The constitution is so perfectly military, that even the postal service is managed by soldiers. At each station a subaltern officer receives the pass for post-horses and examines it, another soldier puts horses to, a third greases the wheels, and a fourth mounts the box. Whenever the uniform is seen, the peasant stops, stands at ease,

and brings his body into a military posture. The
regularity, rapidity, politeness, with which travellers
are served, forms the best proof of the value of mar-
tial discipline.

It may be easily imagined that the introduction of
this system was accompanied by excessive difficulties,
and it was received by the countrymen with great
repugnance. Their mode of life was remodelled;
inmates were forced upon them; their sons were
bound to remain in the colony, and subject themselves to strict military discipline, while their daughters were forced to marry within the limits of the
colony. The next generation, which was educated in
a thoroughly military fashion, reconciled themselves
to this state of things. As Russia contains nearly
six millions of crown serfs, the whole army could be
easily colonised. But in the colonists, assistants, cantonists, and lads, it possesses a school, which is never
drawn dry, and from which this immense army is
constantly supplied with recruits, accustomed from
their earliest years to the use of weapons. The formerly gloomy and silent villages are now cleanly,
freshly built, and converted into military settlements,
where signal-posts, watch-houses, and numerous pat-
rols, alternate. The prettily-painted posts, with gilt
edges and inscriptions, stand on the highway at
regular intervals. If we enter a peasant's house, we
do not find the usual filth of the Russian cabins, but
the greatest military cleanliness and order. The
military villages have excellent streets, generally
paved; on each side are ditches, and trees have been
planted.

(1.) MILITARY COLONIES IN NEW RUSSIA :—2

grenadier divisions, 1 light division of grenadier cavalry, 1 guard artillery brigade, 1 grenadier sapper battalion, 1 instructing sapper battalion, 1 grenadier tirailleur battalion, 1 instructing carbineer regiment.

(2.) MILITARY COLONIES IN NEW RUSSIA:—1 cavalry reserve corps.

(3.) MILITARY COLONIES IN THE UKRAINE:—The 2d cavalry corps, 1 light cavalry division, 1 horse artillery brigade.

(4.) MILITARY COLONIES IN KIEV AND PODO-LIA:—9 light cavalry divisions, 9 horse artillery brigades. The total strength of the military colonies may be estimated at 80,000 men, with 200 guns.*

REMARKS.—Recruiting without substitution, but with right of purchasing discharge (1000 rubles paper) in quotas of fourteen, estate-holders, &c., the higher classes, enjoying exemption; under the banners serfs become free; defective *cadres* of officers by the reserve, as they must be detached from the active army on the mobilisation of the reserve; the 2nd reserve is commanded by pensioned officers. The corps of officers is partially filled up from the military educational establishments, and a great portion of them possess no theoretical information. There is also great favouritism in promotion; and the Russian staff and adjutancies are filled up with a number of men of inferior worth. The army is also badly

---

* We do not believe that Russia at the present time can bring into the field more than 500,000 men of all the forces described above. The Crimea, &c., may be occupied by 160,000 to 180,000 men, Poland and the interior by 120,000, the Baltic provinces by 100,000 to 120,000, and the Caucasus by hardly 80,000 men.

provisioned, owing to the systematic venality and cheating, more especially perceptible in the remote provinces. No non-commissioned officer can be promoted to officer's rank, &c.

THE RUSSIAN NAVY.

(1.) NAVAL GENERAL STAFF OF THE EMPEROR.

The staff is made up as follows:—

1 chief.
1 dufour-general.
1 master of the ordnance of the reserve artillery.
1 inspector of the corps of the naval architects.
1 chief of the marine chancery.
2 adjutants-general.
4 vice-admirals.

In addition, are attached to the Emperor's personal suite—

2 rear-admirals.
2 wing-adjutants.
3 captain-lieutenants.

(2.) MINISTRY OF MARINE.

1. The admiralty council, composed of 10 admirals.
2. The marine auditory-general (1 president and 5 clerks).
3. The naval chancery (3 clerks).
4. The ministerial chancery (2 clerks).

To the department of the Marine Ministry are attached—

1. The inspections (1 vice-admiral, with 6 officers).
2. The hydrographical department (1 lieutenant-general).
3. The medical department (1 director-general).
4. The audit department (1 auditor-general of the fleet).
5. The fortress department (1 engineer-general).
6. The marine training department (1 admiral and 8 members).
7. The marine intendancy (1 lieutenant-general, with 4 members).
8. The marine commissariat department (1 councillor).
9. The shipbuilding department (1 vice-admiral).
10. The timber department (1 major-general).
11. The marine artillery department (1 master of the ordnance).

(3.) THE FLEET.

This is composed of 2 divisions of equal strength—the Baltic fleet, and the fleet of the Black Sea—in 5 divisions; 3 stationed in the former sea, 2 in the latter.

Russia possessed, before the siege of Sebastopol, the following vessels, exclusive of ships building, and the flotillas in the White, Caspian, and Ochotsk Seas :—

4 ships of the line, of 120 guns.
6   „   „   100   „
26   „   „   80 to 90 guns.
18   „   „   70 guns.
48 frigates, of 44 to 60 guns.
50 corvettes, brigs, and schooners.
34 steamers.
350 gun-boats, &c.

This fleet was manned by about 42,000 sailors, and 20,000 marines and artillerymen, of which the greater portion, however, were not specially adapted for the naval service. The fleet carried about 9000 guns.

The actual strength of each division was :—9 ships of the line, of 84 to 120 guns ; 6 frigates, 14 corvettes and brigs, 8 steamers, &c. Hence, the Russian Baltic fleet would consist of 27 ships of the line, 18 frigates, 42 corvettes and brigs, as well as 24 steamers, and we may calculate from 200 to 300 gunboats as belonging to it. Still, according to accurate statements, only 18 of these ships of the line could keep the sea ; and of other vessels, only 9 frigates, 8 brigs and corvettes, 10 paddle-wheel steamers, but not a single screw. The Black Sea fleet, which might be regarded, owing to its geographical position, as in better order than the Baltic, comprised, in 1853—

5 ships of the line of 120 guns.
13   „   „   80   „
7   „   „   54   „
3   „   „   40 to 80 guns.
25 brigs, corvettes, &c., with 170   „
2 steam corvettes, each of 6 guns, &c.

Twenty years ago, the Russian fleet only amounted to one-half this complement; but, at the present moment, owing to the number of ships sunk before Sebastopol, the Black Sea fleet may be regarded as quite innocuous.

It is estimated that a Russian ship only lasts two-thirds of the time of an English vessel, which is assumed to last twenty years. (The building is generally bad, and, in the Black Sea, the vessels are injured by a worm which is very prevalent near Sebastopol). There is also a great deficiency in screw steamers; but Russia has striven, during the last few years, to remedy this defect.

IV.

THE TURKISH ARMY AND NAVY.

THE TURKISH ARMY.

SINCE the year 1843, the Turkish army was composed, on the French-Prussian system, of the following quotas :— (1.) The regular active army; (2.) the reserve ; (3.) the auxiliary contingents ; (4.) the irregular troops.

SUPREME COMMAND.

1 commander-in-chief (seraskier), at the same time Minister of War.

1 supreme council of war (dari churaï), with 1 chief, a member of the Ulmia, to attend to the judicial department. 2 feriks, or lieutenant-generals, and 4 assistants (commander-in-chief of the reserve, inspectors of the artillery depôts, the manufactories and military schools, as well as several other higher officers and adjutants).

1 master-general of the ordnance and inspector of fortresses, under whom are 12 special departments —fortresses, war *matériel*, powder mills, manufactory of small arms, foundries, artillery and engineers, as well as a few less important branches. This office is quite independent. It has immediately under it—

4 regiments of fortress artillery, the engineers, and the separate corps in Crete, Tunis, and Tripoli.

I. THE REGULAR ACTIVE ARMY (NIZAM).

This is formed of 6 corps or orders, each in 2 divisions (commanded by 2 feriks), or 6 brigades (commanded by 6 livas or major-generals). The orders are commanded by mushirs or field-marshals ; have their own staffs composed of 1 ferik, 1 chief, 1 major-general, and several other general officers, and are immediately under the orders of the seraskier. They are recruited in regular districts, from which they draw their reserves.

$$1 \text{ order.} \begin{cases} 6 \text{ regiments infantry.} \\ 4 \quad\quad\text{ „ }\quad\quad \text{cavalry.} \\ 1 \text{ regiment artillery.} \end{cases}$$

All the orders, consequently, amount to 36 regiments infantry, 24 regiments cavalry, and 6 regiments artillery.

1. INFANTRY (FRENCH MODEL).

1 infantry regiment is composed of 4 battalions (tabur), of 8 companies (buluk), and, at its full strength, is made up of—

> 1 colonel (mîr alaï).
> 1 lieutenant-colonel (caimacam).
> 1 major (alaï emini).
> 4 commandants of battalions (bim bachi).
> 4 adjutants (kolassi).

32 captains (yuz bachi).
64 lieutenants (mulazim).
32 sergeant-majors (bach tchāvouch).
128 sergeants (tchāvouch).
32 farriers (buluk emini).
256 corporals (on bachi).
96 musicians (mehter).
32 water-carriers (sakka).
8 surgeons (djerrah).
4 assistant surgeons (etchzaji).
8 field-preachers (imâm).
2560 rank and file (neffer).

Hence, 1 infantry regiment amounts to 3260 men, and a company, of 1 captain, 2 lieutenants, 1 sergeant-major, 4 sergeants, 3 musicians, and 81 men; but, on the average, a regiment has only a strength of 2800 men.

2. CAVALRY (FRENCH MODEL).

The Turkish regular cavalry are armed and mounted alike, and are all light cavalry.

Each cavalry regiment is divided into 6 squadrons, of which 2 are chasseur and 4 lancers.

Strength of a squadron—1 first captain, 1 second captain, 1 first lieutenant, 1 second lieutenant, 1 shoeing smith, 6 sergeants, 18 busadiers, 2 trumpeters, 110 mounted, and 10 unmounted soldiers. Altogether—151 men.

Strength of a regiment—1 colonel, 1 lieutenant-colonel, 1 major, 2 chefs d'escadron, 1 adjutant, 2 surgeons, 2 saddlers, 4 shoeing smiths, 2 field chaplains = 934 men. Here, too, the effective strength

is considerably less, as 1 cavalry regiment amounts to
only 736, or the squadron to 120 men.

3. ARTILLERY (PRUSSIAN MODEL).

In addition to the 6 regiments attached to the 6
orders, there are 4 other artillery regiments, namely
—1 reserve regiment, and 3 regiments for service in
the fortresses, the Dardanelles, &c., and in the Bos-
phorus.

1 regiment = 6 horse, and 9 foot batteries, of
1500 men, with 60 field guns; among them, 4
mountain howitzers. The howitzers (long and short)
are collected in separate batteries. The whole artillery has at its disposition above 1600 guns of various
calibres, exclusive of the fortress *matériel*. Of these,
only 360 are attached to the active army, and above
1200 to the reserve.

The strength of an order, consequently, amounts to
20,980 men, with 60 guns.

4. THE ENGINEER CORPS (FRENCH MODEL).

The engineers are divided into 2 regiments, each
of 800 men, and organised exactly like the French.
Like the corps of 16,000 men, detached to Tunis and
Tripoli, it forms a component of the orders.

Hence, the actual strength of the regular Turkish
army will be as follows:—

36 regiments	infantry	=	100,800	men.
24 "	cavalry	=	17,280	"
7 "	field artillery (including 1 reserve)	=	9,100	"
3 "	fortress artillery	=	3,900	"
2 "	engineers	=	1,600	"
8 "	detached corps	=	16,000	"

Total, 148,680 „

The actual war establishment should be somewhat larger than the above figures.

II. THE RESERVE (REDIF).

After five years' service, the active part of the army enters the reserve for seven years' further service, their strength and organisation being exactly correspondent with those of the active troops. The orders of the reserves are decided according to the recruiting districts, and always have the requisite number of permanently paid officers and non-commissioned officers, as well us ample depôts of arms, &c., at head-quarters, so that the reserves can be speedily called out to exercise. The manœuvres, during which the reserves receive pay, &c., like the Nizam, usually take place once a year for a month.

III. THE AUXILIARY CONTINGENTS.

According to the new regulations, all the tributary, but not yet subjugated provinces furnish the following quotas :—

1. Danubian principalities .	6,000	men.
2. Servia	20,000	,,
3. Bosnia and the Herzegowina	30,000	,,
4. Upper Albania . . .	10,000	,,
5. Egypt	40,000	,,
6. Tunis and Tripoli . .	10,000	,,

Total . 116,000 men.

The Danubian principalities can furnish altogether
3 regiments infantry, 2 regiments cavalry, with 1
battery, or about 6,800 regular troops, and about
61,000 militia; in Servia there is a similar proportion;
and Egypt, in case of need, can bring into the field
above 100,000 excellent troops, exercised according
to the European pattern.

IV. IRREGULAR TROOPS.

1. Mussulman volunteers, at least . .	50,000	men.
2. Gensdarmerie (foot, cavass, horse, sujmen) and rural police (subashi) . . .	6,000	,,
3. Tartars of the Dobrudza, and immigrant Cossacks of the Don	5,500	,,

Total, 61,500 ,,

The irregular troops, however, could, in case of
need, be raised to a much larger amount.

Total strength of the Turkish army:—

148,680 regular troops.
148,680 reserve.
116,000 auxiliary contingents.
61,500 irregulars.

Total 474,860 men.*

* At the present moment Turkey has at least 300,000 men in the field,

We may, however assume, that only one half these numbers may be regarded as ready to take the field, as not only is the regular army generally beneath its actual strength, but the reserves, auxiliary contingents, and irregular troops cannot be correctly estimated. Some of the contingents must always be regarded as uncertain; as, for instance, the troops of the Danubian principalities, Servia, Tunis, and Tripoli; but, on the other hand, the Egyptian force can be mobilised in a very short period.

The strength of the army has been kept up since 1844, partly by volunteers, partly by ballot, which generally brings 25,000 men under the banners, each order having its special district. The exceptions are the same as in France. Since the above date the Turkish government has begun to take into the army those Christians who freed themselves by paying the Kharadz (capitation tax), a very important measure, which has lately been universally introduced, as the Mohammedan population of Turkey scarcely amounts to three-fifths of the whole.

Among the military educational establishments in Turkey, we may mention—the imperial military school, from which about 100 cavalry and infantry officers are annually drawn; further, 6 other schools, serving as preparatory schools to the above, and 1 attached to each order; the artillery and engineers' schools; and, lastly, the naval school. But for all that, these schools are not sufficient to educate a large portion of the officers, and many of them are utterly deficient in a scientific education. In addition, great

which amount will probably be kept up for some time, or so long as she can procure money for their pay and maintenance.

attention is devoted to regimental education, which is imparted by the clergy. At any rate, the great amelioration introduced into the Turkish army by the Tanzemat, is most remarkable.

The commissariat department is generally good.

The armament of the infantry consists of muskets and bayonets, (they carry no baggage, but it is transported on beasts of burden). The cavalry, lances and sabres.

THE TURKISH NAVY.

1 minister of marine (kapudan pacha).

1 admiralty council (medshlici khairie) ; 1 president and seven members.

The fleet has :—

     1 kapudan pacha.
     5 admirals (fehriki khairie).
     3 vice-do. (kapudana beg).
     8 rear-do. (reala beg).

In the year 1853, Turkey had :—

2 ships of the line, 1st class, of 120 to 130 guns.
4   ,,   ,,   2d   ,,   74 ,, 90   ,,
10 sailing vessels,   40 ,, 60   ,, .
 6 corvettes,   22 ,, 26   ,,
14 brigs,   17 ,, 20   ,,
16 schooners, cullus, &c.,   4 ,, 12   ,,
 6 steam frigates, of 450 to 800 horse-power.
12   ,,   corvettes and smaller vessels.

Total, 70 ships, with about 34,000 sailors and artillery, 4000 marines, and 3000 guns, to which we must add the Egyptian fleet, with a strength of 4 ships of the line, 4 frigates, 5 war steamers, and the requisite number of smaller vessels.*

1 ship of the line, of 74 to 130 guns, has—1 commandant (beg), 1 second commandant, 16 officers, 1 chaplain, 3 surgeons, and from 700 to 900 men, &c. on a war establishment. Ships of 74 guns have 600 men; those of 52 to 64 guns, 300 to 500 men; corvettes from 18 to 44 guns, 150 to 200 men; and brigs of 12 to 18 guns, 100 to 150 men.

* At Sinope the Turks lost 7 frigates, 2 corvettes, 1 steamer, 2 transport ships, and 1 gunboat, part of them being Egyptian.

THE GREEK ARMY.

WE will close this section of our work with a few
details about the insignificant forces which Greece
can bring into the field. The land forces comprise,
according to the latest organisation, a general staff
of 57 officers, 6 line and 3 chasseur battalions, of
6 companies ; with 237 officers; altogether = 6636
men in peace, and 9873 men on a war establishment. 1 battalion artillery, of 4 companies, or 6
batteries, with 19 officers = 365 men; 1 lancer
regiment, of 6 squadrons, with 10 officers = 269
men ; 2 pioneer companies, with 280 men ; the
phalanx (noble guard), with 410 officers ; gensdarmerie, frontier troops, and invalids, with 170 officers
= 4000 men. Altogether = 11,960 men.

The fleet consists of—2 corvettes, of 26 guns ; 2
steamers, one mounting 6 guns ; 3 brigs, of 12, 10,
and 2 guns ; 7 schooners, of which 2 mount 10 and
26 guns ; 5 cutters, 12 gunboats, with 22 guns.
There is also a marine artizan company, of 78
men.

V.

SARDINIAN ARMY AND NAVY.

THE SARDINIAN ARMY.

THE COMMAND IN CHIEF.

1 marshal, 3 generals, 12 lieutenant-generals, 24 active, 5 disposable, and 6 honorary major-generals.

GENERAL STAFF.

Inspectors of the army—3 generals; corps of the general staff—1 general, 39 officers; general staff of the military divisions—5 generals, 20 officers; general staff of the fortresses and provinces—215 officers, 41 men.

THE ARMY.

INFANTRY.

Line infantry—10 brigades = 20 regiments, of 4 battalions, or 16 companies.

1 company = 78 non-commissioned officers and men.

1 regmnt. { 1 commander of the regiment (colonel or lieutenant-colonel), 4 majors, 2 adjutants, 1 paymaster, 1 sub-ensign, 1 field chaplain, 1 regimental, 2 battalion surgeons, 16 captains, 16 first-lieutenants, 32 lieutenants, 1276 non-commissioned officers and men. } = 1353 men.

Strength of the line infantry = 27,100 men.

Tirailleur corps (*bersagleiri*) = 10 battalions, of 4 companies, and 1 depôt company.

1 company = 93 non-commissioned officers and men.

10 battalns. { 1 colonel, 1 lieutenant-colonel, 10 majors, 1 captain, commissariat; 1 staff-captain, 1 paymaster, 1 commissariat officer, 1 inspector of *matériel*, 2 lieutenants, 1 regimental adjutant, 10 adjutants of battalions, 1 regiment and 9 battalion surgeons, 40 captains, 81 first-lieutenants, 82 lieutenants (1 first-lieutenant, and 1 lieutenant for the depôt company), 3833 non-commissioned officers and men. } = 4077 men.

Total strength of the infantry = 31,177 men.

Armament—line infantry, like the French; the bersagleiri armed with short Delvigne Tyrolese rifles.

CAVALRY.

9 regiments of 5 squadrons, including 1 depôt squadron, of which 4 are line, and 3 light cavalry regiments.

1 squadron = 141 non-commissioned officers and

men ; 1 depôt squadron = 18 non-commissioned officers and men.

1 regmnt.	1 colonel or lieutenant-colonel, 1 major, 1 captain of commissariat, 2 adjutants, 1 paymaster, 1 commissariat officer, 1 field chaplain, 1 regimental, 1 battalion surgeon, 2 assistant-surgeons, 5 captains, 9 first-lieutenants, 9 lieutenants, 600 non-commissioned officers and men.	= 635 men, with 542 horses (without depôt).

Total strength of cavalry = 5715 men.

ARTILLERY.

Committee of direction—corps staff, and 3 artillery regiments.

The committee of direction is composed of 3 generals.

Corps staff.	1 colonel, 1 lieutenant-colonel, 6 majors, 11 captains, 23 subalterns, 59 non-commissioned officers and men.	= 101 men, with 20 mules.

Artizan regiment (8 companies).	1 colonel, 1 lieutenant-colonel, 2 majors, 2 adjutants, 1 paymaster, 1 commissariat officer, 1 staff-officer, 1 field chaplain, 1 regimental, 1 battalion surgeon, 13 men. In the 8 companies, 8 captains, 15 first-lieutenants, 9 lieutenants, 448 men.	505 men, 74 horses.

Fortress regiment.	1 colonel, 1 lieutenant-colonel, 2 majors, 2 adjutants, 1 paymaster, 1 commissariat officer, 1 staff officer, 1 field chaplain, 1 regimental, 1 battalion surgeon. In the companies, 12 captains, 24 first-lieutenants, 12 lieutenants, 1048 non-commissioned officers and men.	= 1108 men.

Field regiment (10 brigades, or 20 companies).	1 colonel, 1 lieutenant-colonel, 7 majors, 2 adjutants, 1 commissariat officer, 1 staff officer, 1 field chaplain, 1 regimental and 2 battalion surgeons, 2 assistant-surgeons, 20 captains, 40 first-lieutenants, 20 lieutenants, 2098 non-commissioned officers and men.	= 2197 men ; 1016 horses.

The field regiment (10 batteries).	6 foot batteries, each 6 6-pounder guns, and 2 7-pounder howitzers. 2 horse batteries, each of 6 6-pounder guns, and 2 7-pounder howitzers. 2 batteries of position, each of 8 12-pounder guns.

Hence, each battery will contain 8 guns. The foot batteries have 4, all the others 6 horses.

Total strength of the artillery corps = 3811 men, with 80 field guns.

ENGINEER CORPS.

1 council — staff and direction — 1 regiment of pioneers. 2 generals, 1 of whom is chief of the staff, the other, commandant of the corps.

Council—4 colonels or lieutenant-colonels.

Staff—2 colonels or lieutenant-colonels, 6 majors, 22 captains, 7 first-lieutenants, 1 lieutenant.

The regiment of pioneers.	1 colonel or lieutenant-colonel, 2 majors, 10 captains, 1 paymaster, 2 adjutants, 1 commissariat, 1 staff officer ; 20 first-lieutenants, 10 lieutenants, 1 chaplain, 1 regimental surgeon, 1 battalion do., 1065 non-commissioned officers and men.	= 1159 men.

TRANSPORT CORPS.

4 compies. { 1 colonel or lieutenant-colonel as commandant ; 1 major, 1 adjutant, 1 commissariat officer, 1 paymaster, 1 director of the transport column, 1 regimental surgeon, 1 veterinary do., and 14 men. 4 captains, 4 first-lieutenants, 8 lieutenants, 440 non-commissioned officers and men. } = 474 men.

CARBINEER CORPS.

Horse and foot carbineers. { 1 general, 1 colonel, 2 lieutenant-colonels, 4 majors, 21 captains, 30 first-lieutenants, 12 lieutenants, 2 adjutants, 1 quartermaster, 1 regimental surgeon, 1 battalion do. 833 non-commissioned officers and men (horse) ; 2338 non-commissioned officers and men (foot carbineers). } = 3248 men ; 620 horses.

LIGHT CAVALRY.

(*Island of Sardinia*).

1 colonel, 1 lieutenant-colonel, 2 majors, 1 officer of commissariat, 1 staff officer, 1 supernumerary lieutenant, 1 regimental surgeon, 3 squadron surgeons, and 3 veterinary do. = 34 men.

6 squadrons = 6 captains, 12 first-lieutenants, 6 lieutenants, 1050 non-commissioned officers and men = 1074 men.

Light cavalry total = 1122 men, 741 horses.

SANITARY AND DISCIPLINARY COMPANIES.

In the sanitary service—98 officers and 352 men are employed.

5 punishment companies = 644 officers and men.

The total Sardinian army would, consequently, amount to about 47,600 men, with 80 guns; which, if necessary, could be doubled, by calling in the reserves.

REMARKS.—Universal service, from the twentieth year, in two classes; either in the *ordinanza* for 8 years uninterruptedly, or in the *provinziali*, where the soldiers are bound to serve for 6 years (2 in the reserve), but are only periodically called out. Substitution is permitted.

THE NAVY.

PERSONNEL OF THE FLEET.

1 admiral.
1 vice-do.
3 rear-do.
7 captains of ships of the line.
6 captains of frigates.

The total strength amounts to 2860 men.

FLEET.

1 ship of the line, of 64 guns.
1 frigate,   61 ,,
3 steam do.,   48 ,,
2 corvettes,   44 ,,
4 brigs.
1 brigantine.
1 gabarra.
8 gunboats.
8 steamers, with 1690 horse-power.

Total, 29 vessels, with 405 guns, 22 carronades, and 1690 horse-power.

VI.

THE AUSTRIAN ARMY AND NAVY.

THE AUSTRIAN ARMY.

IT is indisputable that Austria possesses, at the present moment, an army inferior to none other in Europe, not only in strength, but in perfect efficiency. Formerly, a system of routine, involving only antiquated forms, prevailed; and the defects it necessarily produced, can be estimated from its working in our own Crimean army. The troops of Austria, during the campaigns of the French Revolution, were constantly defeated—not from any lack of bravery, but owing to the fatal system of regulating the military movements in Vienna, and rendering the commanders subordinate to the supreme council of war. The Hungarian Revolution purified the army from the majority of its defects, and the incessant activity of the youthful Emperor has placed it on a footing which all must regard with honest admiration.

Every arm of the service has been improved by the new organisation, and a spirit of confidence animates every soldier, high or low. It must not be forgotten, that it was this confidence imparted by

Frederick the Great and Napoleon to their troops, that enabled them to gain many of their most celebrated victories. At the same time, every attention has been paid to the education of the officers of the line, who have hitherto been comparatively inferior to the artillery and engineers. In short, wherever we turn we find that every exertion is being made to put the Austrian army on a most efficient footing; and if Austria is not impeded by being forced to take part in the war prematurely, she will be enabled to carry all her cherished designs into effect.

The staff of the Austrian army is thus composed:—

ADJUTANTS OF THE EMPEROR.

Adjutants-general.
{ 2 lieutenant field-marshals.
{ 1 major-general.

Wing adjutants.
{ 1 colonel.
{ 2 lieutenant-colonels.
{ 1 major.

Adjutants.
{ 1 captain (cavalry).
{ 2 captains (infantry).

THE MILITARY CENTRAL CHANCELLERIE OF THE EMPEROR.

2 lieutenant field-marshals.
1 major-general.
1 colonel.
1 lieutenant-colonel.
2 majors.
1 captain (infantry).
1 captain (cavalry).
1 first-lieutenant.

THE SUPREME COMMAND OF THE ARMY.

(Formerly Ministry of War.)

This branch contains 4 sections, with the following divisions:—

1st section. { Adjutancy-general, with 1 major-general and 9 officers.

2d section. { Chancellerie of operations, with 1 master of the ordnance and 9 officers.

3d section. { Administration, with 1 major-general, 14 officers, and several employés, divided into 12 departments—chancellerie, recruiting, remounting, invalids, commissariat, sanitary, military frontier, fortification, accounts, and justice.

4th section. { Educational establishments, with 1 major-general and 5 officers.

THE GENERAL DIRECTION OF ARTILLERY AND ENGINEERS.

The former contains one master of the ordnance as president, 21 officers, and various clerks; the latter 1 lieutenant field-marshal, as director general, 75 officers (principally belonging to the staff), and the requisite clerks, both being divided into six departments.

SUPREME MILITARY COURT.

1 master of the ordnance as president; 1 major-

general, vice-president; 5 general auditors and examiners; 4 other clerks.

GENERAL MILITARY COURT OF APPEAL.

1 master of the ordnance as president; 1 auditor-general, 12 colonels, as auditors; 16 clerks.

QUARTERMASTER-GENERAL'S STAFF.

1 quartermaster-general, 1 lieutenant field-marshal, 2 major-generals, 17 colonels, 12 lieutenant-colonels, 22 majors, 40 captains of the first class, and 30 captains of the second class.

THE ETAT MAJOR.

The Austrian army at the present moment counts the following general officers.

	Attached.	Unattached.
Field-marshals . .	6	—
Cavalry generals . .	23	28
Lieutenant field-marshals	116	87
Major-generals . .	160	119
Colonels . . .	254	232

Altogether, about 15,000 officers of all grades.

INFANTRY.

Austria has 77 regiments and 26 battalions of infantry, of which 62 belong to the line, 14 regiments and 1 battalion of border infantry, and 1 regiment and 25 battalions of chasseurs.*

Each regiment of the line contains :—

* As the regiments are more generally known by their names than by their numbers, we will add their titles. (Those titles marked, in this and a subsequent note, with an asterisk are permanent).

I. LINE INFANTRY.—(1.) Emperor Franz Joseph ; (2.) Emperor Alexander I ; * (3.) Archduke Carl ; * (4.) Hoch and Duetsch Meister ; (5.) Prince Edward Liechtenstein ; (6.) Count Coronini ; (7.) General Prohaska ; (8.) Archduke Ludwig ; (9.) Count Hartmann Klarstein ; (10.) Count Mazzuchelli ; (11.) Prince Albert of Saxony ; (12.) Archduke William ; (13.) vacant ; (14.) Ludwig, Grand Duke of Hesse Darmstadt ; (15.) Duke of Nassau ; (16.) Lieutenant Field-marshal Zanini ; (17.) Prince Hohenlohe ; (18.) Constantine, Grand Duke of Russia ; (19.) Prince Carl Schwartzenberg ; (20.) Prince Frederick William of Prussia ; (21.) Count Liningen ; (22.) Count Wimpffen ; (23.) Chevalier von Airoldi ; (24.) Louis Duke of Parma ; (25.) General von Wocher ; (26.) Michael, Grand Duke of Russia ; (27.) Leopold, King of the Belgians ; (28.) Lieutenant Field-marshal von Benedek ; (29.) General von Schönhals ; (30.) Count Nugent ; (31.) Baron von Culoz ; (32.) Duke of Modena ; (33.) Count Gyulay ; (34.) Prince of Prussia ; (35.) Count Khevenhüller ; (36.) Count Degenfeld Schonburg ; (37.) Paskèwitch, Prince of Warsaw ; (38.) Count Haugwitz ; (39.) Dom Miguel ; Lieutenant Field-marshal von Rossbach ; (41.) Baron von Sipkovitch ; (42.) George, King of Hanover ; (43.) Baron von Gippert ; (44.) Archduke Albert ; (45.) Archduke Sigismund ; (46.) Baron Jellachich ; (47.) Count Kinzky ; (48.) Archduke Ernest ; (49.) Baron von Hess ; (50.) Prince of Thurn and Taxis ; (51.) Archduke Carl Ferdinand ; (52.) Archduke Franz Carl ; (53.) Archduke Leopold Ludwig ; (54.) Prince Emile of Hesse ; (55.) Baron von Bianchi ; (56.) Baron von Fürstenwärther ; (57.) Prince Felix Joblonovski ; (58.) Archduke Stephen ; (59.) Archduke Ranier ; (60.) Prince Gustavus of Vasa ; (61.) Count Strassoldo Graffenburg ; (62.) Baron von Tursky.

II. NATIONAL FRONTIER INFANTRY.—(1.) Liccan ; (2.) Ottochan ; (3.) Ogulin ; (4.) Szluin ; (5.) Warasdin Kruetz ; (6.) Warasdin St George ; (7.) Brood ; (8.) Gradiscan ; (9.) Peterwardein ; (10.) First Banat ; (11.) Second Banat ; (12.) German Banat ; (13.) Romani do. ; (14.) Illyrian do. Frontier infantry battalion of Titel.

III. CHASSEURS.—Tyrolese rifle regiment—Emperor Francis Joseph.

1 grenadier battalion.
4 field battalions.
1 depôt battalion.

Each grenadier and depôt battalion has 4 companies, but the field battalions, 6; so that each regiment is composed of 32 companies, of which 8 take the field, and 4 remain at the depôt. Each grenadier and field company, on a full war establishment, is composed of—

1 captain.
1 first-lieutenant.
1 second-lieutenant (1st class).
2 second-lieutenants (2d class).
2 sergeants.
10 corporals.
4 musicians.
2 carpenters.
184 rank and file (16 tirailleurs).

Or, including staff, &c., 220 men.

A depôt company will contain 130 men of all ranks; but, probably, this number will be very irregular, and depend on circumstances.

Hence, including the staff officers :—

1 grenadier battalion	=	884 men.
1 field ,,	=	1324 ,,
1 depôt ,,	=	524 ,,

Or, each regiment of the line, including depôts, will amount to 6,704 men.

The entire strength of the line regiments, conse-

quently, when on a war footing, and all the field and
depôt battalions are at their full depôt strength, will
amount to 415,648 men.

62 battalions = 248 companies of grenadiers,
or 54,808 men.
248 field battalions = 1,488 companies, or
327,352 men.
62 depôt battalions = 248 companies.

The whole of the line wear white tunics, with
collars and facings of different colours (in summer
and in barracks, blouses of coarse gray linen are
worn), light blue trowsers (the Hungarian regiments
wear the light Hungarian trowser), long cloaks of
thick light-gray cloth, and a small low cloth cap,
covered with wax-cloth. The arms consist of a
smooth-bored percussion gun, with bayonet; but in
each company there are 16 sharpshooters, armed with
rifles. All the non-commissioned officers, together
with the grenadiers, musicians, and pioneers, wear
short side-arms, the rest merely the bayonet in a
leathern sheath. The knapsacks are very good,
and the belts, to which the pouch and bayonet are
attached, are crossed diagonally on the chest.

THE BORDER INFANTRY.

This arm of the Austrian service is so peculiar
in its nature, that we cannot proceed to furnish its
statistics until we have given a short statement of
the organisation and origin of the military frontier.

" The foundation and development of this institution," Mr Kohl tells us, in his *Reisen Durch Œsterreich*, " began with the fall of the Hungarian kingdom, at the battle of Mohacs (1525), with the accession of the Austrian emperor to the Hungarian crown, and with the beginning of the great war between the Turks and the Germans for the dominion over these Eastern countries, which lasted nearly 200 years. The Emperor Ferdinand, the brother of Charles V., first quartered German troops in those districts of Croatia bordering on Illyria, in order to protect his new kingdom of Hungary against the incursions of the Turks. This garrison afterwards received numerous additions of Servian and Croatian fugitives from Turkey, who were endowed with lands, on condition of serving as military frontier guards against the Turks. In this manner was first organised the military frontier of Illyria, which was afterwards formed into a distinct Margraviate, under the name of the one perpetual generalty of the Croatian frontiers.

" This generalty is the basis and foundation of the whole subsequent structure. The more the conquests of Austria extended in Hungary, the more the frontier lines were lengthened—the more the Christian power became consolidated and strengthened, the greater was the number of Christian fugitives who took refuge on Austrian ground, from the tyranny of the Mohammedan Government. All these fugitives — Uskoks, Croats, Albanians, Macedonians, Servians, and Wallachians—were hospitably received by Austria, and settled, as before, on the waste lands of Slavonia and the Banat, for the defence of the frontier. As more and more provinces were added to the dominions of Austria, the frontier was finally extended to its Eastern boundary, round Transylvania, in the years 1765 and 1766.

" It is probable that, as civilisation and culture spread southward into the Turkish dominions, this living wall of protection against barbarism may gradually become unnecessary, but at present it is very far from being so. The internal disturbances and convulsions of Turkey, and the unsettled state of the Oriental question on the one hand, and the spirit of discontent, the passion for nationality, now so dangerously prevalent in Hungary, on the other, render the preservation of the military frontier of the very highest consequence to Austria. The work here accomplished by Austria, and indeed by all Germany—for it was only by the help of the money and troops supplied by the rest of Germany that the Austrian Government was enabled to found the military frontier—has been of the greatest service, not merely to Germany, but to all Europe ; for it was this effective and permanent institution which alone formed a rampart against the Turks, and preserved Europe from that dreadful disease to which it was so long subject, and which still rages through the East."

The border infantry consists of 14 regiments, each composed of 2 field battalions, of 6 companies each, and 1 depôt battalion, of 4 companies, but can be very materially augmented, as was the case in 1848 and 1849, when several regiments had 4 battalions in the field. The strength of a border regiment amounts to 3847 men.

1 colonel.

1 lieutenant-colonel.

1 drummer.

53 artillerymen, to serve 4 frontier guns.

3 battalions.

In each company 2 corporals and 16 sharpshooters are armed with rifles and sword bayonets; the remainder with percussion guns and bayonets.

In addition to these 14 regiments, there is one more, called the Titel frontier battalion; so that the strength of the whole border infantry may, at the present moment, be calculated at 55,000 men, recruited along the Austro-Turkish frontier, from the Adriatic as far as Translyvania. They are dressed in brown tunics and black belts, and are of great service as light troops, in skirmishing and patrolling. In fact, they may be regarded as the Austrian Cossacks.

The military portion is divided into two districts; the Croato-Slavonian (Agram), and the Banato-Servian (Temesvar). They have a peculiar form of government; the country is divided into brigades, regiments, companies, and households, the last of whom receive tracts of land as military tenures, on condition that they will provide a certain contingent, armed, accoutred, and paid by Government. They are bound to service, from 20 to 50, in the field, and till their 60th year in domestic service. In peace, they serve as *douâniers*, and occupy the frontier in a strength of from 6000 to 12,000 men, who reside in strong block houses, where they are relieved every ten days. In war, their number is uncertain, but an idea may be formed from the fact that, in 1849, though only

bound to furnish a contingent of about 13,000 men
to the active army, in 1848 they marched 120,000
combatants upon Vienna.

THE CHASSEURS.

The chasseurs consist, *imprimis*, of the Imperial
Chasseur regiment, which is only recruited from natives of the Tyrol. It contains 7 battalions, altogether amounting to 28 companies, and, in addition,
3 depôt companies. Its entire strength, on a war
footing, is 6,864 men.

Secondly: Chasseur battalions.—5 battalions of
6, and 20 battalions of 4, field companies, or altogether, 25 battalions of 110 field companies, with 15
depôt companies. (Since 1849, 13 new chasseur battalions have been formed). A chasseur company, on
full war footing, is composed of:—

        4 officers.
        4 upper chasseurs.
        12 lower chasseurs.
        20 leaders of the rounds.
        2 carpenters.
        2 trumpeters.
        160 chasseurs.

The whole strength of these chasseurs with their
regimental depôts is, upon the war footing, 32,500
men. They are excellently armed with rifles and
sword bayonets. Their uniform consists of tunic and
trowsers of light-gray cloth, with light-green facings,
and a round hat, with the border turned up on one
side, which is far from being ugly. Their belts are
black. They are all chosen men and good shots, and

are selected from the various line regiments. They form excellent patrolling troops, and are well adapted for any description of out-post duty.

GARRISON AND DISCIPLINARY COMPANIES.

(1.) Two cordon battalions in the Bukowine, of 1870 men.

(2). 4 garrison battalions, about 1800 men in each battalion, or together, 32,000 men.

(3). 6 disciplinary companies, whose strength varies with circumstances. These have been only recently established, and are an imitation of the French and Prussian companies of the same description.

From the above cursory statement, it will be seen what strength the Austrian infantry possesses, when placed on a war footing. At least 300,000 excellently drilled line infantry, 25,000 borderers, and the same number of chasseurs, or together, 350,000 excellent troops, can be always employed on foreign service, without in any way weakening the depôts or the garrisons in the fortressess and larger towns of the monarchy.

THE CAVALRY.

The cavalry have always held a high place in the Austrian army, and recent alterations have, if possible, improved this branch of the service. The long time of service (8 years without interruption) rendered it possible to convert them into well trained and disciplined troops, and the abundance of heavy horses in

Bohemia and Moravia, and of light, hardy horses in Hungary, Gallicia, and the Bukowine, greatly facilitates the re-mount system.

The cavalry regiments, by their recent organisation, have been formed into two divisions; the heavy, or German, and the light, or Hungarian, amounting altogether to 40 regiments : 8 cuirassier and 8 dragoon regiments of the former; 12 Hulan and 12 hussar regiments of the latter.*

THE GERMAN CAVALRY.

(1.) The dragoon and cuirassier regiments are formed of 3 divisions = 6 field and one depôt squadron. On a full war footing each squadron is made up of—

---

* I. CUIRASSIER REGIMENTS.—(1.)Emperor Franz Joseph; (2.) Maximilian Joseph II., King of Bavaria; (3.) *vacant*; (4.) Emperor Ferdinand; (5.) Emperor Nicholas of Russia; * (6.) Count Wallmoden Gimborn ; (7.) Duke William of Denmark ; (8.) Prince Carl of Prussia.

II. DRAGOONS. —(1.) Archduke John; (2.) King Louis of Bavaria; (3.) Emperor Franz Joseph ; (4.) Grand Duke Leopold II. of Tuscany; (5.) Prince Eugene of Savoy; * (6.) Count Ficquilmont; (7.) Prince Windischgrätz; (8.) Grand Duke Ferdinand of Tuscany.

III. HUSSARS.—(1.) Emperor Franz Joseph; (2.) Grand Duke Nicholas of Russia; (3.) Prince Carl of Bavaria; (4.) Count Schleck ; (5.) Field-marshal Count Radetzky; (6.) King William I. of Wurtemberg ; (7.) Prince Henry LXIV. of Reuss; (8.) Elector William I. of Hesse Cassel ; (9.) Prince Franz Liechtenstein ; (10.) King Frederick William III. of Prussia; * (11.) Prince Alexander of Wurtemberg; (12.) Count Haller von Hallerköe.

IV. HULANS.—(1.) Count Civilart ; (2.) Field-marshal Prince Carl Schwartzenberg ; * (3.) Archduke Charles Louis ; * (4.) Emperor Franz Joseph; (5.) Count Wallmoden Gimborn; (6.) Emperor Franz Joseph ; (7.) Archduke Charles Louis ; (8.) Archduke Ferdinand Maximilian ; (9.) Prince Carl Liechtenstein; (10.) Count Olam Gallas; (11.) Alexander Emperor of Russia ; (12.) Ferdinand, King of the Two Sicilies.

1 first-captain.

1 second-captain.

4 lieutenants.

2 sergeants.

12 corporals.

1 trumpeter.

174 men.

Or, 194 combatants, with 170 horses.

The strength of the depôt squadrons is very irregular, but it may be assumed that it amounts to 120 to 130 men, so that an entire cuirassier regiment, with staff, &c., will amount to 1200 men.

(2.) The 8 dragoon regiments are of the same strength and divisions as the cuirassiers.

In this way, the whole heavy cavalry of 16 regiments of 96 field squadrons, will amount to 19,000 men, without depôts, who can march into the field. These regiments are recruited from Bohemia, Moravia, Upper and Lower Austria, and Illyria; but not at all from the Tyrol, Hungary, Italy, Dalmatia, Transylvania, and the military frontier. The uniform consists of helmets with brass crests, white tunics with coloured collars, and blue trowsers; and, with the cuirassiers, a bullet-proof cuirass of black polished iron. The principal arm of the heavy cavalry is a long straight cut-and-thrust sabre, with a basket hilt; fifteen men of the squadron are armed with rifled carbines, and one pistol, the remainder with two pistols. Saddles and bridles are excellent. The cuirassier horses are stout and heavy, those of the dragoons, for which a much lower price is paid, are much lighter, and not so strong.

The light cavalry consists of—

(1.) 12 regiments of Hulans. Of these, 8 new regiments have been formed since 1850, by converting 6 chevaux-legers into Hulans, and forming 2 new regiments; one Slavonic and one Italian. Each Hulan regiment is formed of 4 divisions = 8 field squadrons, and 1 depôt squadron. Each squadron, on the complete war footing, is composed of 6 officers and 221 non-commissioned officers and men, with 200 horses. A depôt company may be estimated at 172 men, with 143 horses. The strength of a regiment may, therefore, be taken at 1808 men, with 1596 horses, which will give the total strength of the 8 Hulan regiments at about 22,000 men.

Six or seven of these regiments are recruited exclusively from Gallicia, and attempts are being made to augment this number, as the Poles are famous for the employment of the lance. The horses are also generally drawn from Gallicia and the Bukowine, Moravia and Bohemia. The arms consist of a sabre, and a lance with a black and yellow pennon. 16 men per squadron have rifled carbines and 1 pistol, the remainder 2 pistols. The uniform is green kurtkas with red collars, and yellow epaulettes and shoulder-straps, green trowsers with a broad red stripe, and coloured schakos, forming a tasteful *ensemble*. The cloaks are made of white cloth, like the remainder of the Austrian cavalry. The Hulans are first-rate troops, and their value was so fully proved in 1849, that any augmentation of them is most desirable.

(2.) 12 regiments of hussars, entirely recruited in Hungary and Transylvania, and mounted on the light horses of those countries, which are admirably adapted for hussars. The strength and organisation of a hussar regiment is precisely similar to that of the Hulans. These Hungarian hussar regiments, which have been entirely remodelled since 1849, have gained such renown in every war, that it would be superfluous to say more in their praise. The uniform, materially altered since the insurrection, consists of dark blue attilas with lace, narrow Hungarian trowsers of the same colour, czishenis, and very low-crowned schakos. The hussars are armed with sabres, and one half carry rifled carbines and one pistol, the remainder a smooth-bored carbine and pistol.

The imperial army, consequently, when on a war footing, can muster 19,264 heavy, and 63,392 light cavalry, or, altogether, 62,500 men, without counting the reserves in depôt. Let us assume that a portion of these must remain in garrison, we may calculate that at least 50,000 can be sent into the field for a campaign in an enemy's country. This cavalry is so excellently organised that it need not fear comparison with any other European army, and in a war carried on in a level country, would be of inestimable advantage.

THE ARTILLERY.

The artillery forms the third branch of the Austrian army. Since 1849, it has been augmented and re-organised, and one special improvement we may mention is, that the drivers form part of the artillery, instead of being attached to the transport corps. Great improvements have also been made in the *ma-*

teriel, and the whole arm is now in an extraordinary degree of efficiency.

The artillery, in addition to the staff, is divided into field,* fortress, and technical artillery.

(1.) The field artillery, by the latest organisation, is made up of 12 regiments. Each regiment, on a war footing, having 3 12-pounder foot batteries, each of 8 guns; 4 6-pounder foot batteries of 8 guns; 1 long howitzer battery of 8 guns; and 6 horse batteries of 8 guns.

(2.) A rocket regiment of 20 batteries, which are served by 3865 artillerymen, and 2466 horses.

(3.) A coast artillery regiment: 20 companies with 3447 men, who are principally employed in the defence of the coast.

A 12-pounder battery on a war footing has—

> 4 officers.
> 31 non-commissioned officers of all grades.
> 2 trumpeters.
> 71 drivers.
> 84 gunners.
> 130 horses.

A 6-pounder battery has the same number of officers, but only 66 gunners, and 65 drivers, with 118 horses.

---

* The chiefs of the *field artillery regiments* are :—(1.) Emperor Franz Joseph ; (2.) Archduke Louis ; (3.) Baron von Augustin ; (4.) Lieutenant Field-marshal von Haustab; (5.) Lieutenant Field-marshal von Sturtnik; (6.) Archduke William ; (7.) Prince Luitpold of Bavaria ; (8.) Major-general Baron von Smold ; (9.) Major-general Chevalier von Pettinger ; (10.) Lieutenant Field-marshal von Berwaldo ; (11.) Major-general Chevalier von Fitz : of the *rocket regiment,* Baron von Augustin; the *coast artillery regiment,* Major-general Baron von Stein.

A horse-battery, 50 gunners, 91 drivers, and 166 horses.

The fortress artillery, as its name indicates, is employed in the fortifications, and is made up of 8 battalions of about 10,400 men.

The technical artillery is composed of—

(1.) The ordnance department in the foundries, &c., with 12 laboratory companies = 2200 men.

(2.) The rocket and pyrotechnic company of 480 men.

(3.) The rifle-makers' company of 360 men.

(4.) The artificers' company of 1600 men.

The whole strength of the Austrian artillery, on a war footing amounts, therefore, to about 48,000 men, who can bring into the field nearly 1100 guns. But, even assuming that only 32,000 men with 1000 guns can be employed, this is in itself a very large number.

The artillery uniform consists of dark-brown tunics with red collars and facings, blue trowsers, and a round felt hat with a black-yellow brush. The men are armed with a short sword suspended from a bandalier of white leather. The horses are principally derived from Bohemia, Moravia, and Austria, and though not large or handsome, are compact, powerful, and lasting.

THE ENGINEERS.

The engineers form the fourth arm of the service, and are divided into the staff, and the troops ; the former containing 220 officers. The engineers form a regiment of 3 field battalions = 18 companies, and 1 instructing battalion of 6 companies ; its entire strength, on a war footing, amounting to 5380 men, three-fourths of whom are sappers, and one-fourth miners.

In addition, four battalions of pioneers = 14 companies, who are also instructed in pontooning. A battalion amounts to 1376 men, or the whole corps to 5600 men.

The uniform of the pioneers is gray and green, very like that of the chasseurs. The first two ranks are armed with short rifles, the third with serrated sabres.

To the pioneer corps is also attached the flotilla founded in 1849, and stationed on Lake Garda, the Danube, the Po, and the Lagunes of Venice : it is made up of 8 companies, composed of 1500 men, who man 10 little steamers and 50 tugs.

The entire strength of these troops, on a war footing, will therefore amount to 12,000 men, of whom we may assume that 10,000 can be brought into the field. The officers, generally, are well educated, and the troops excellently instructed.

There are also attached to the Austrian army 3 sanitary corps, of 14 companies, amounting to about 3460 men. These troops were formed in 1848, on the French pattern, and will be indubitably of great service in war. They perform their duties in the ambulances, field hospitals, &c.; and the men are specially instructed for that object.

In war, a corps of estafettes is established, principally selected from old pensioned soldiers. They serve as escorts in reconnoitring, &c., and number 377 men, who are divided among the various corps d'armée.

We also find 2 divisions of staff dragoons, selected from the best riders who have been discharged, and intended to serve as orderlies to the various staffs. In war, too, 2 battalions of staff infantry are called out, amounting to about 1200 men. All these regulations, principally introduced by F. M. Radetzky in the Italian army, are intended to prevent that selection of the best men in the regiments as orderlies, which is found so detrimental to the service.

There is a special transport corps to horse the ammunition columns and baggage waggons of the army, composed of 43 divisions. Its strength varies greatly, and cannot, therefore, be stated; but, at any rate, it is amply sufficient for the service; the horses are generally strong and active, and obtained from Bohemia and Moravia.

The gensdarmerie, founded in 1849, must also be regarded as forming part of the army, as it is recruited from discharged soldiers of good character. It forms 20 regiments, with about 400 officers of all grades, and about 19,000 gensdarmes; the sixth part of whom are mounted. They are well paid, and handsomely dressed—forming a very fine corps, of great service in maintaining order throughout the empire.

The Austrian army has no guards' brigade, but each regiment possesses equal privileges and duties with the other. Those guards called the Arcieren

Leib Garde, Trabanten Leib Garde, Leib Garde Gensdarmerie, and Hofburg Wache, altogether do not amount to more than 400 men, principally veterans, and employed in guarding the monarch and the palaces.

RECAPITULATION.

300,000 grenadiers and line infantry.
25,000 border infantry.
25,000 chasseurs.
50,000 cavalry (one half heavy).
32,000 artillery, with 1000 guns.
10,000 pioneers, sappers, miners, &c.
8,000 sanitary troops, estafettes, orderlies, staff battalions, &c.

450,000 men, without the transport corps, all excellently equipped, and animated with the best spirit. In addition, 200,000 men of the various arms would be left at home in the fortresses, chief cities, frontier districts, and depôts. These 450,000 men, when taking the field, could therefore be always kept up at the war standard, without stripping the country of troops required for its internal defences.

THE AUSTRIAN NAVY.

THE MARINE SUPREME COMMAND.

This is divided into 7 department—presidial, military, shipbuilding and equipment, machinery, marine artillery, commissariat, paymaster and judicial.

In addition to the commander-in-chief and his *ad latus* (rear-admiral), there is an admiralty board, composed of 7 members.

ADMIRALTY.

1 rear-admiral, as commandant.
1   „   (inspector of fleets and brigadier of marines).
8 captains of ships of the line (colonels).
10   „   frigates (lieutenant-colonels).
10   „   corvettes (majors).
29 lieutenants of ships of the line (captains, 1st class).
21   „   frigates (captains, 2d class).
11 ensigns of ships of the line (first-lieutenants).
48   „   frigates (second-lieutenants).
87 marine cadets.

The other troops and *personnel* belonging to the fleet are:—the corps of sailors; the marine artillery —1 commandant, 26 officers, to manage embarkations; and the technical artillery; the regiment of marines —1 colonel, 1 lieutenant-colonel, 2 majors, and 46 other officers; the corps of shipbuilders and engineers —20 surgeons, 5 auditors, 5 chaplains, and 124 civil officers.

STATE OF THE FLEET.

	Schwarzenberg	60 guns.
	Bellona	50 „
6 frigates.	Novara	42 „
	Venus	32 „
	Radetzky (building)	31 „
	Juno (towing ship)	10 „
	Carolina	24 „
	Diana	24 „
6 corvettes.	Leipzig	20 „
	Minerva	14 „
	Titania	12 „
	1 corvette (building)	22 „
	Montecuculi	
	Orestes	
	Pilades	
7 brigs.	Pola	16 „
	Trieste	
	Triton	
	Hussar	
	Elizabeth	12 „
	Phœnix	12 „
5 goelettes.	Arethusa	10 „
	Artemisia	10 „
	Saida (building)	8 „

2 praams (Mongebello and Vesuvius), each of 12 guns; 1 mortar vessel (Saetta), of 10 guns; 34 peniches, each of 3 guns; 18 gun-boats, each 4 guns; 5 schooner brigs, each 4 guns; 9 tenders and 11 steamers; Custozza (6 guns); Lucia (7 guns); Volta (6 guns); Elizabeth (4 guns); Alnoch (2 guns); and the steam-yacht Seamen.

STRENGTH OF THE AUSTRIAN MARINE:—104 ships and vessels, with 784 guns, of which 1 propeller frigate, 1 propeller corvette, 1 goelette, and 1 steamer, are either building or being equipped. The head-quarters of the fleet are at Trieste.

VII.

THE PRUSSIAN ARMY AND NAVY.

THE PRUSSIAN ARMY

MUST be regarded from a very different stand-point from that of Austria, for, in forming our opinion of it, and more especially of the Landwehr system, whose opponents are very many, we must bear in mind, before all, that Prussia exerted all her energies to form an army of half a million of combatants, in spite of her population only amounting to 16,000,000, and her extremely unfavourable geographical position; for this was her only method to maintain a position as a European great power. If we keep this in mind, we cannot refrain from expressing our admiration of all the Prussian military arrangements, for, considering the slight means at her command, she has worked wonders. In fact, a succession of great men was requisite to give an army, recruited from only 16,000,000 souls, that European importance which Prussia has succeeded in retaining even to the present day. The first founders of Prussia's military power were the Great Elector, and the strict Frederick William I., who converted their country into one huge camp. Frederick the Great worthily completed what his predecessors had so well commenced, and his brilliant victories first implanted in the Prussian army that military pride which now distinguishes it in so eminent a degree. After the death of this great king and general, the government was satisfied in retaining the empty form without the animating spirit which had so brilliantly distinguished it hitherto. They closed their ears obstinately to the requirements of the age, and would not perceive that with Napoleon I. a new chapter in the strategic art had commenced. The defeat at Jena, and the following days of misfortune — although many regiments fought bravely, and did not disgrace the old reputation of Prussian courage —were the necessary consequence of such insane blindness. The Prussian army, and with it the Prussian states, might easily have been ruined, had not Providence given them men who were enabled to form again a compact whole out of the fragments. All that was good in the old school was retained, the bad and antiquated was rejected, and a new organisation was substituted, possessing the highest merit. Above all, Scharnhorst, whose name will endure as long as a Prussian soldier wears his cockade with honour ; then Boyen, Gneisenau, Clausewitz, York, Grollman, and Blücher, and many others, were the founders of the present Prussian *esprit de corps.* "It must be regarded as an honour through the whole nation to be allowed to wear the soldier's coat—a disgrace not to be considered worthy of it." Such, in a few words, is the basis of the spirit which has enabled Prussia to keep her military dignity till now unweakened. Every son of the nation must feel a pride in being allowed to become a combatant for it ; and had not this feeling been kept up, Prussia would never have re-attained her place in the European family.

The new organisation prospered, however, spite of the unspeakable difficulties it had to contend with, both abroad and at home,—thanks to the spirit which created it, and the powerful will of the Prussian nation, which instinctively recognised its importance. The sanguinary years of 1813 to 1815 furnished the army with an opportunity for action, and it displayed itself in the brightest colours. We are perfectly aware that the Prussian Landwehr battalions and the youthful volunteers would have fared much worse, had not the old well-disciplined French regiments been lost in Russia, and their place taken by raw conscripts, but still their services were most meritorious. The Prussian Landwehr acquired an honourable name both from friend and foe in those campaigns, and we feel sure that they will always do their utmost to retain it.

After gaining many blood-stained laurels, the Prussian army returned home, and afforded a striking proof of the value of the new organisation. And, although a certain reactionary party—horrified at the institution of the Landwehr with its bourgeois officers, and regarding it as an insult that the son of a count must perform his military duties alongside the tailor's apprentice as a private—tried hard to upset it; fortunately, any overthrow of the new system had by this time been rendered impossible. It was far too deeply implanted in the Prussian nation, and the calm, reasoning mind of Frederick William III. was too cognizant of its value to allow any important alterations to be carried

into effect. It is true that much was introduced
between the years 1828 and 1842 which did not
quite harmonise with the spirit of a Scharnhorst;
but the fundamental principle remained unaltered,
and was even more jealously protected than before,
when Boyen was appointed Minister of War. The
events of 1848 and 1849 have given no extraordinary
impulse to the Prussian organisation, but showed
once more what an excellent spirit generally per-
vaded the army. It withstood many and severe
trials, but always did its duty, and proved itself a
thoroughly-disciplined and well-affected force. Great
and widely-extending alterations have been effected
since 1851, by attaching the Landwehr still more
closely to the line, and by appointing regular officers
to the command of the militia battalions. We regard this as a very great improvement; for, though
thoroughly recognising the immense value of the
Landwehr, and especially the spirit which animates
it, we undoubtedly believe that its efficiency has been
greatly augmented by a closer attachment to the
line. General von Bonin, who founded his reputation by the formation of the Schleswig-Holstein
army, has gained no slight credit in Prussia by the
introduction of these regulations.

But what causes us more especially to admire the
Prussian army, is the spirit of military pride which
animates nearly all the troops. The remembrance
of the glorious past, and the certainty that no one
can be a soldier who has committed a dishonouring
crime, but that every soldier can lay claim to honourable treatment at the hands of his superiors, produced
this proud sentiment. Had it not been so—had the

troops been regarded as mere machines—the revolution of 1848 would have found willing instruments in the Prussian army, and the troops would not have withstood the corrupting influences which would have subverted the throne. Another admirable point is the high degree of education which all the officers enjoy. The excellent military schools, and the severe examinations to which officers are subjected with the greatest display of impartiality, have produced this highly-desirable result. The non-commissioned officers are also remarkable for a great degree of instruction and excellent temper. The military spirit which, thanks to the establishment of universal service under arms, animates a large majority of the Prussian nation, displays in this instance again its valuable results. After these rapid allusions—for they could not be more, as any full explanation would naturally have led us far afield—we will pass to the composition of the Prussian army.

ADJUTANTS OF THE KING.

1. general-adjutants.
   { 3 generals of infantry.
   { 2   „   cavalry.
   { 3 lieutenant-generals.

2. wing-adjutants.
   { 5 colonels.
   { 3 lieutenant-colonels.
   { 1 major.
   { 2 captains.

Attached to the suite :—2 major-generals.

THE MINISTRY OF WAR

is divided into 2 departments and several sections.

K

I. General War Department.—5 divisions as follows :—

(1.) Division for the affairs of the army (food, mobilisation, dislocation, substitution, &c.)

(2.) Division for affairs of the artillery (artillery depôts, provision of the army with arms, powder-mills, &c.)

(3.) Division for the engineers.

(4.) Division for the marine.

(5.) Division for personal affairs.

In addition to these, the secret war chancery.

II. The Department of Military Administration, containing three divisions—

(1.) Division for the exchequer and staff.

(2.) Division for uniform, commissariat, and train.

(3.) Division for hospital service, &c.

In addition, the invalids, re-mount, auditor-general, and military chest departments, are under the Minister of War.

GENERAL COMMANDS AND INSPECTIONS.

Next to the Ministry of War come the 9 general commands of the guard and the 8 corps d'armée, as well as the general inspections of the artillery (4 inspections), of the engineers and pioneers (3 inspections), of fortresses (6 inspections), and the inspection of chasseurs and rifles. A general command is composed of the commander-in-chief of a corps d'armée and a staff, formed of a general staff and adjutancy (in peace 1 staff officer and 1 captain in each), the intendancy (1 intendant with 4 assistants), the auditor of the corps, the surgeon-general of the corps, and the military chaplain's department (4 sections). A general inspection is similarly composed of the inspector-general and the requisite staff and adjutants ; and an inspection is composed of the inspector with his adjutants.

Among the administrative authorities we may mention—

(1.) The intendancies under the authority of the commissariat department (by each corps d'armée 1).

(2.) The auditory-general, as highest court of military justice, made up of 1 auditor-general, 4 chief auditors, &c.

(3.) The military chaplains' department (1 field dean as chief authority, under him the chaplains of the corps d'armée, the division chaplains, &c.)

(4.) The garrison administration under the orders of the intendancy (barracks, Landwehr depôts, guardhouses, &c.)

GENERAL STAFF.

This is divided into the Great General Staff, and the General Staffs of the Corps d'Armée, amounting, in peace, to about 50 officers. The former must be acquainted with the organisation of their own

army, as well as those of other states. It contains,
in addition, the map and plan office, the topographical and trigonometrical division, as well as the
lithographic institution. The staff of the army corps
consists of—

Corps staff.
{
1 general or lieutenant-general, commanding
   corps (with 2 aides-de-camp).
1 colonel (chief of staff).
1 major (sub-chief).
1 intendant (commissary).
4 deputy-intendants.
1 assessor (jurisprudence).
1 auditor (judge-advocate).
1 staff-surgeon.
1 chaplain.
}

Divisional
staff.
{
2 lieutenant-generals, commanding divisions
   (each 2 aides-de-camp).
4 auditors.
2 Evangelical } chaplains.
2 Catholic   }
6 major-generals, commanding brigades (1 aide-
   de-camp each).
}

THE INFANTRY.

The infantry is composed of the guards, the line,
the Landwehr of the first and second levy.

The guards contain 4 regiments = 12 battalions
= 48 companies ; 1 reserve regiment of guards =
2 battalions = 8 companies ; 1 chasseur and 1 rifle
battalion of the guards, together amounting to 8
companies. A company of the guards is made up
of—

5 officers.
1 ensign.
18 non-commissioned officers.
1 doctor.
4 musicians.
2 train soldiers.
227 rank and file.

258

A battalion, exclusive of officers and staff, contains 1002 men, and a regiment 3006. The whole infantry of the guard, consequently, amounts to 16,032, without officers, &c.

The two battalions of chasseurs and rifles are armed with the Thouvenin chasseur rifles; the other battalions entirely with the now so celebrated needle-gun. The guards are chosen from the tallest and picked men in the kingdom. They have distinguishing marks on their collars and helmets, better bands, and enjoy several other privileges The officers of the first regiment of guards and of the *garde du corps* receive double pay; but, with this exception, the pay and rank of all grades are precisely similar to those in the line. A regiment of the guards certainly presents a grander appearance on the parade-ground than one of the line, and this is especially the case in the cavalry; but the future will teach us whether they would be of more service in the field. In the campaign of 1813 to 1815, the guards were only twice under fire—namely, at Möckern and Paris—and displayed that bravery which may be justly expected from every Prussian regiment.

The line infantry is composed of 32 regiments,
each regiment of 2 musketeer and 1 fusilier battalion;
8 so-called reserve infantry regiments, each made up
of 2 musketeer battalions; and 8 combined reserve
battalions, 1 attached to each corps d'armée; or
altogether to 120 battalions : each battalion on a
war footing containing 1002 men, without officers
and staff.   The entire line infantry would consequently amount to 120,240 men, without officers, &c.
The 32,000 fusiliers, for whom light and active men
are selected, are armed with needle-guns, the remainder with smooth-bored percussion muskets.   In
consequence of the universal conscription, the Prussian
infantry regiments can call in many more soldiers on
furlough than their strength requires, and, therefore,
during a protracted war, they could always be kept
up to their full establishment.

In addition, we must mention 8 battalions of chasseurs, each battalion = 4 companies = 1002 men,
exclusive of officers and staff, or altogether 10,016
men.   These chasseur battalions are armed with
Thouvenin rifles, are generally chosen, as far as
possible, from practised marksmen and foresters'
sons ; and they are always kept in a perfect state
of efficiency.

The entire line and guards would, therefore, have
148,292 rank and file.   Of these, 36,000 are fusiliers
and 10,000 chasseurs, or altogether about 46,000
light troops.   With the exception of the 8 reserve
battalions, which are intended during war to form
depôts, the whole of the line and guards infantry
are ready for service in the field, and very con-

siderable reserves can be held in readiness at home.

The uniform consists of blue tunics with red collars and facings (the chasseurs, green tunics and felt caps), long gray pantaloons, dark-gray cloaks, and the well-known *pickelhaube* or helmet of leather, with metal ornaments. The belts, arms, knapsacks, &c., are all in excellent condition, and of good patterns; and we may safely assert that the Prussian line infantry wants for nothing which could increase its efficiency.

We also consider the Landwehr of the first levy, especially since its recent re-organisation, equally well prepared for war. Each line regiment has now 1 Landwehr infantry regiment attached to it, bearing the same number and forming a brigade with it. Thus, for instance, the first line and the first Landwehr regiment form the first infantry brigade.

The Landwehr of the first levy contains 4 Landwehr regiments of the guard = 12 battalions; 32 Landwehr regiments, of 3 battalions = 96 battalions; 8 Landwehr battalions of the reserve regiments, or, altogether, 116 battalions, of the same strength and composition as those of the line, or 116,032 rank and file. They are perfectly equipped and organised for immediate service in the field. The 8 battalions of the reserve would alone be kept back for service in the garrisons. The Landwehr infantry wear the same uniform as the line (except the red edging on the tunic, and that on the front of the helmet there is a cross with the motto, "With God for King and Fatherland"), and are armed with percussion muskets, a bayonet, and side-arms. The staff-officers and leaders of companies of the first levy are entirely drawn from the line, but the lieutenants are either officers who have retired, or those men of the educated classes, who formerly fulfilled their military duties by serving one year in the line or guards, and then passed an examination as Landwehr officers. The first levy is drawn from men between twenty-six and thirty-two years of age, who have already served their time in the line. But, as the number of these men would be too great, many exceptions from this general rule occur. During a time of peace, the Landwehr of the first levy is only called out once every two years, when they go through their manœuvres for several weeks with the line regiments.

The chasseurs have no actual Landwehr attached to them, but each battalion, when marching into the field, calls in enough men on furlough to form a fifth company, called the reserve, so that 2½ battalions of chasseurs would remain behind.

According to these regulations Prussia could, therefore, employ in a foreign campaign :—

12	battalions of guards	= 12,024	men.
12	„ guards Landwehr	= 12,024	„
96	„ line infantry	= 96,192	„
96	„ Landwehr (first levy)	= 96,192	„
10	„ chasseurs	= 10,020	„
262	„	= 226,452	„

For garrisoning the numerous fortresses, chief towns, formation of depôts, there would be left in addition to the Landwehr of the second levy :—

1 guard reserve regiment	= 2 battalions	=	2,004	men.
8 line „ „	= 16 „	=	16,032	„
8 Landwehr „		=	8,016	„
36 line depôt battalions		=	36,072	„
Chasseur reserve	= 2½ „	=	2,500	„
Or, 64½ battalions		=	64,624	„

It is indubitable that, in case of need, a large portion of the latter troops could be sent into the field. The military organisation of Prussia is of such a nature, that from 280,000 to 290,000 excellently-disciplined and thoroughly-equipped infantry troops can always be employed beyond the frontiers of the country. Of course, such exertions must not last any great length of time, for they would prevent the cultivation of the ground, and disturb the regular relations of commerce.

In addition to the Landwehr of the 1st levy, the 2nd levy is made up of 116 infantry battalions = 82,900 men. This levy is not intended to be employed in an external war, but is amply sufficient for garrisoning fortresses and disciplining recruits, &c. The officers are generally selected from those who have retired on a pension, or have obtained civil employment; and the rank and file are men between thirty-two and thirty-nine years of age, who have also served. During peace the second levy is not called out; but in the autumn of 1850, they were generally under arms. The numerous evils detected on this occasion the government has been since earnestly engaged in removing. This 2nd levy will never be converted into parade troops, but they will perform all that is required of them, and that is the main point. At the present time the arms and accoutrements of the 2nd levy are all in readiness, which was not the case in 1850.

THE CAVALRY.

The Prussian cavalry are also divided into the guards, the line, and the Landwehr.

The guards and line cavalry are made up as follows :—

10 cuirassier regiments (2 belonging to the guards) = 40 squadrons. On a war footing each of these regiments will be composed of

    1 colonel.
    1 staff-officer.
    6 captains (2 attached to the Landwehr).
    4 first-lieutenants (ditto, ditto).
  12 second ditto.
    4 cornets.
  89 non-commissioned officers.
616 men, or

744 men, with 702 horses (without officers).

The Prussian cuirassiers wear white tunics, gray trowsers, metal helmets, and white or yellow back and breast-plates. They are armed with a long, straight cut-and-thrust sword ; in addition, each man has a pistol, and 20 in each squadron carbines. Their horses are tall and handsome, and are generally obtained in the Eastern provinces of the empire, namely, East and West Prussia, and Pomerania.

The total strength of the cuirassiers is equal to 7410 men, who are all intended to take the field.

The Prussian guard and line Hulans are mounted on horses very like those of the Austrian dragoons, and form the transition from light to heavy cavalry. There are 2 guard and 8 line Hulan regiments, made up precisely like the cuirassiers, and, therefore, amounting to 7410 men. The horses of the Hulans, of whom a regiment is attached to each corps d'armée, are very good, and not so slenderly built as those of the hussars and dragoons. Their arms consist of a lance, with a black and white pennon, and a sabre; 20 men per squadron have carbines, the remainder a pistol. The uniform is dark-blue jackets, with red collars and facings, and dark-gray trowsers and cloaks, such as are worn by the entire Prussian cavalry.

The light cavalry is made up of—(1.) 13 regiments of hussars (1 belonging to the guards). Each regiment is of the same strength as the preceding, or, altogether, 9633 men, all intended for active service. Their principal weapon is the sabre, and, in addition, two-sevenths carry short rifles, four-sevenths carbines, and one-seventh pistols. The uniform consists of dolmans and fur jackets of various colours, a bearskin cap with a colpak, gray trowsers and cloaks.

(2.) 5 regiments of dragoons (among them 1 of dragoon guards), altogether amounting to 3705 men. The dragoons are mounted and armed precisely like the hussars, and are only distinguished from them by the uniform, which consists of a light-blue tunic and a helmet of leather, with brass ornaments.

The light cavalry horses are chiefly obtained from East and West Prussia and Lithuania, and are generally very good and handsome, though here and there some of them are not sufficiently strong.

The strength of the whole guard and line cavalry is, consequently,—

40	squadrons	cuirassiers	=	7410 men.
40	,,	Hulans	=	7410 ,,
52	,,	hussars	=	9633 ,,
20	,,	dragoons	=	3705 ,,
				,,
152				28,185 ,,

who are all employed on active service.

(1.) 2 guard Landwehr regiments, each regiment of 4 squadrons, with 602 horses, or, altogether, 2408 horses. The men are chosen from those who have served their time in the guards, and, when called out, are generally commanded by old officers of the same branch. A portion of these guard Landwehr cavalry, whom we had an opportunity of seeing in 1850, was most admirably equipped and drilled, and might fearlessly challenge comparison with any regiment of the line.

(2.) 8 heavy regiments of Landwehr cavalry = 32 squadrons = 4816 men. These heavy regiments are made up with men who have served their time in the 8 line cuirassier regiments, and are attached to them in such a manner that 1 heavy Landwehr and 1 cuirassier line regiment are commanded by the same colonel.

(3.) 8 Landwehr Hulan regiments = 32 squadrons = 486 men, also attached to the 8 line Hulan regiments, and armed, like them, with lances.

(4.) 12 Landwehr hussar regiments = 48 squadrons = 7224 men, attached to the 12 line hussar regiments.

(5.) 4 Landwehr dragoon regiments = 16 squadrons = 2408 men, attached to the dragoon line regiments.

The total Landwehr cavalry of the first levy will, therefore, amount to 136 squadrons, or, on a war footing, 20,416 horses. The whole of this Landwehr cavalry of the first levy, intended for service in the field, can always be called out within a few weeks, as all the *materiel* is ready, with the exception of horses. The officers and men have all served for various periods in the cavalry of the active army, and find themselves perfectly at home in their military duties very soon after being called out. The re-mounting of this Landwehr cavalry varies, rather, as this is generally effected in that province to which the Landwehr regiment belongs. In East and West Prussia, Lithuania, several districts of Pomerania, Brandenburg, Silesia, Saxony, and Westphalia, where a good breed of horses is kept up, the Landwehr cavalry is excellently mounted; in the Rhenish provinces and some districts of Westphalia, Silesia, and Saxony, this is not exactly the case. Some time must, besides, always elapse before a newly called out Landwehr regiment of cavalry is thoroughly disciplined and organised. But when this has once taken place, and the regiments have passed a few months in the field, they would not be in any way inferior to a line regiment. They are all armed like the line. The uniform

consists of a dark-blue tunic, with different collars
and facings, according to the various arms, and a light
helmet of the dragoon pattern.

The Prussian cavalry intended to be employed in
an external war would consequently be made up of—

28,158 men, line and guards.
20,416 Landwehr cavalry (first levy).
_____

48,574 men, thoroughly equipped.

In addition to these 34 Landwehr regiments of the
first levy, there are 8 reserve squadrons, appointed to
serve in the fortresses. Whenever the army is on a
full war establishment, 55 depôt squadrons will be
formed, with a total strength of 6350 horses. These
reserves and depôts will have a strength of 7000 or
8000 men and horses, and are sufficient to keep up
the field regiments at their full strength.

The Landwehr cavalry, second levy, is intended to
be made up of 104 squadrons, each squadron of 120
horses, or altogether, 12,480 combatants. We do
not doubt that by an extraordinary exertion the whole
of the second levy could be mobilised, but we believe
that, otherwise, it would present great difficulties.
They would not be employed except in case of an
invasion of the country, and though they would have
many defects they would still be of some service to
the state.

THE ARTILLERY.

The artillery of the Prussian army is composed of

9 artillery regiments, of which 1 is attached to the guards.

Each regiment is made up of 3 detachments, each commanded by a staff officer, and is composed of—

4	6-pounder foot batteries, of 8 guns	=	32	guns.
3	12-pounder „ „ 8 guns	=	24	„
1	7-pounder howitzer battery, of 8 guns	=	8	„
3	horse 6-pounder batteries, of 8 guns	=	24	„
11 batteries with			88	„

In addition, each regiment has 1 fortress artillery detachment, 1 reserve company, 1 artisan company, 1 laboratory column, and 6 ammunition columns. On a war footing each regiment will be made up of—

5 staff-officers.
21 captains.
15 first-lieutenants.
50 second do.
3 pyrotechnic do.
1374 non-commissioned officers and privates.

There is no actual Landwehr artillery, but each regiment has Landwehr artillery officers and men attached to it, who are called out to exercise in time of peace, and in war would be employed to reinforce the regiment and serve the fortress ordnance. In addition to the artillery, the Prussian army has numerous arsenals, foundries, and powder-mills, which are all under military management, and served by soldiers.

The strength of the artillery intended to take the field is 19,000 men, with 99 batteries of 792

guns. In comparison to the general strength of the
Prussian army, this number of field guns appears
rather small. Recent strategics attach a great weight,
and we believe justly, to heavy batteries. It seems
as if Prussia had recognised this defect, for it has
lately been stated that each artillery regiment is to be
augmented by a battery, which would form an addi-
tional total of 9 batteries, equal to 72 guns, and hence
864 guns will be brought into the field in future.
But even this number is not sufficient, and it ought
to be raised to at least 900, with as many 12-pound-
ers as possible. Since small arms have been so
greatly improved during the last ten years, we believe that it will be necessary to introduce guns of
much heavier calibre than the 6-pounders which are
now so much in vogue. The French artillery, which
is an object of special attention, has set a good ex-
ample in this.

If there was a period when the Prussian artillery
was treated in a rather step-motherly fashion, every
exertion has been made since 1848 to repair the error,
and it is now on a very satisfactory footing. The
officers, educated in excellent schools, combine theoretical knowledge with practical experience, the men
are well disciplined, and the *materiel* is excellent.
The horses are powerful animals, which are principally
bought up in the eastern provinces. As in all else,
the guards have a preference here, and their horses
are considerably superior to those of the line artillery.

The uniform is a dark blue tunic with black collars
and facings, a helmet of leather with brass ornaments,
trowsers and cloaks dark-gray.

THE ENGINEERS.

The engineer corps, with the pioneers, who must also perform the duties of pontonniers, contains 216 officers, and 9 pioneer detachments (1 belonging to the guards) ; each detachment has 2 companies, and contains 452 men. In war, a depôt company of 225 men is to be formed of the Landwehr men of the pioneer detachments. There are also 2 reserve pioneer companies, together amounting to 500 men, attached to the Federative fortresses, which Prussia helps to garrison. The total strength of the pioneers on a war footing, after calling out the Landwehr pioneers, will amount to 7743 men. As Prussia has many strong fortresses, not more than 5000 pioneers could be detached for a foreign campaign. This number appears rather small. The general condition of these troops is declared by competent military authorities to be extremely satisfactory, and we could not indeed expect otherwise in so intelligent an army as the Prussian.

The Prussian army on a war footing would also have the following corps attached :—

(1.) A transport corps, subdivided into various detachments. On a war footing it would amount to 27,000 men, and its organisation is most praiseworthy.

(2.) Mounted orderlies, especially attached for carrying despatches, &c., 4 officers and 77 men.

(3.) An army corps of gendarmerie, attached to the various staffs, whose number is not settled.

(4.) A company of non-commissioned officers of the guards, of 80 men, who serve in the royal palaces and gardens.

As the organisation of the Prussian army is especially calculated upon the intelligence of the officers and men, all the military educational establishments are, and always have been, excellent. For officers the following schools have been founded :—

Five cadet houses.
Numerous divisional schools for preparation of ensigns.
An artillery and engineer school.
A general war school for the higher instruction of officers.

In addition to the regimental and company schools, we also find :—

Schools for non-commissioned officers.
A military orphan school, with branches through the country.

For the purpose of introducing a regular system of equitation in the cavalry there is a military riding-school at Schwedl, and an instructive battalion for infantry at Potsdam. The various regiments detach competent officers and soldiers to join these establishments.

The whole Prussian army, including the Landwehr of the 2nd levy and the reserves, would have a strength of 580,000 men. Of these there might be employed in a campaign beyond the frontiers of the country :—

Guard, line and Landwehr infantry (first levy)	226,452	men.
Guard, line and Landwehr cavalry (first levy)	48,574	„
Artillery (exclusive of the present augmentation), 792 guns, with .	19,000	„
Engineers, officers, and pioneers .	5,000	„
	299,026	„

Or, in round number, 300,000 effectives.

The Prussian army during peace is divided into a corps of guards, permanently garrisoned in Berlin, Potsdam, and Charlottenburg; and into eight corps d'armée, one to each province. Each corps d'armée is composed of

4 line infantry regiments.
4 Landwehr do. do. (1st levy).
1 chasseur battalion.
4 line cavalry regiments.
4 Landwehr do. do. (1st levy).
1 regiment artillery.
1 pioneer division.
1 combined reserve battalion.

The eight reserve infantry regiments, of which each corps d'armée has one, are principally garrisoned in Mayence, Luxemburg, Frankfort-on-the-Maine, and on the Rhine. As the Prussian regiments during peace very rarely change their garrisons, which would, indeed, entail various difficulties, owing to their close connexion with the Landwehr, the division into divisions and brigades may be regarded as permanent, but would probably be entirely altered on the troops taking the field.

THE PRUSSIAN NAVY.

In 1854, Prussia was in possession of the following vessels :—

1 sailing frigate (Gefion) . . .	18	guns.
1 steam corvette (Danzig) . . .	12	„
1 „ „ (Barbarossa) . .	10	„
1 exercising ship (Amazon) . .	12	„
2 paddle-wheel avisos (Salamander and Nix)*	12	„
1 paddle-wheel transport (Preussescher Adler), of 310 horse-power . .	4	„
1 sailing transport (Mercury) . .	4	„
2 schooners	6	„
36 gun-boats (2 guns each) . . .	72	„
6 gun-yawls	6	„
52 vessels.	190	„

The *personnel* amounted to 1180 men, with 66 officers; but in war it could be raised to 3120.

REMARKS. — The Prussian Government intends within ten years to build 12 frigates, of 60 guns; 10 screw corvettes, of 8 to 12 guns; 14 avisos, of 6 to 8 guns; 5 schooners, 3 to 4 guns; 5 exercise and transport vessels; 36 gun-boats, and 6 yawls;—or, 88 new ships.

The regulations for the organisation of the Prussian marine, published 7th July 1854, are as follows :—

The navy is divided into the following sections :—

* Since exchanged with the English Government for the ' Thetis frigate.

1. The marine *personnel* contains—(1.) the corps of naval officers and cadets; (2.) the sailors; (3.) the deck officers; (4.) the dockyard corps; (5.) the sea battalion; (6.) the marine staff; (7.) the hospital assistants; (8.) the marine engineers; (9.) the paymaster's department; (10.) the naval chaplains; (11.) the naval auditors; (12.) the naval surgeons.

2. The *personnel* of the fleet is divided into seamen, comprising naval officers and cadets, petty officers and sailors; and landsmen, to which all the other persons belong.

The naval officers and cadet corps contains the following charges :—

    (1.) Admiral (with general's rank).
    (2.) Vice-admiral (lieutenant-general).
    (3.) Rear-admiral (major-general).
    (4.) Captains (colonels).
    (5.) Captains of corvettes (majors).
    (6.) Lieutenants, first class (captains).
    (7.)   „   second class (first-lieutenants).
    (8.) Naval cadet, first class (second-lieutenants).
    (9.)   „   second class (porte l'épée ensigns).
  (10.) Volunteer cadets.

To enter as volunteer the following conditions are required :—(1.) age not beyond 15; (2.) good health; (3.) passing a satisfactory examination in mathematics and science.

VIII.

ARMY OF THE CONFEDERATION.

THE

ARMY OF THE CONFEDERATION.

By the regulations drawn up by the Diet in 1842,
each federative state of Germany is bound to furnish
one per cent. of its entire population, as simple contingent to the army of the confederation; two weeks
after mobilisation, one-third per cent. as reserve; and
one-sixth per cent. to provide for casualties; or, altogether without trains, one and a-half per cent. The
strength of the federative army is thus made up :—

    1. Simple contingent (including the garri-
        sons of the fortresses)   .   .   . 303,493 men.
    2. Reserve and supplement   .   .   . 151,767 „

                           Total, 455,260 „

These forces are divided into ten corps d'armée, and
one reserve infantry division of 13 battalions, as follows :—

I. SIMPLE CONTINGENTS.

Corps d'armée.	Divisions.	States.	Infantry.	Cavalry.	Artillery and Train.	Pioneers and Pontoniers.	Total.	Guns.
I., II., III., IV., V., VI., VII. VIII.	6 6 2 1 1 1	Austria	73,501	13,546	6,827	948	94,822	192
		Prussia	61,629	11,355	5,705	795	79,484	160
		Bavaria	27,566	5,086	2,592	356	35,600	72
		Wirtemberg	10,816	1,994	1,005	140	13,955	28
		Baden	7,751	1,429	720	100	10,000	20
		G. D. Hesse	4,802	885	446	62	6,195	12
		Total of 8th division	23,369	4,308	2,171	302	30,150	60
IX.	1	Saxony	9,302	1,714	864	120	12,000	24
		E. Hessen	4,402	811	409	57	5,679	12
		Nassau	3,721	...	281	37	4,039	8
		Total of 9th division	17,425	2,525	1,554	214	21,718	44
		Garrison of Luxemburg	1,869	362	280	25	2,536	6
X.	1 1 1	Hanover	10,118	1,865	940	131	13,054	28
		Brunswick	1,625	299	151	21	2,096	4
		Holstein Lauenburg	2,791	514	259	36	3,600	8
		Mecklenburg-Schwerin	2,775	511	258	36	3,580	8
		Mecklenburg-Strelitz...	588	71	52	7	718	2
		Oldenburg	2,650	...	157	22	2,829	4
		Hamburg	1,007	185	93	13	1,298	} 4
		Bremen	376	69	35	5	485	
		Lübeck	316	58	29	4	408	
		Total of 10th division	22,246	3,572	1,974	275	28,067	58
	Reserve Infantry Division.	Saxe-Weimar	2,010				2,010	
		Saxe-Altenburgh	982				982	
		Saxe-Coburg-Gotha	1,116				1,116	
		Saxe-Meiningen	1,150				1,150	
		Anhalt Dessau	529				529	
		Anhalt Bernberg	370				370	
		Anhalt Köthen	325				325	
		Hesse Homburg	200				200	
		Waldeck	519				519	
		Schaumburg Lippe	240				240	
		Lippe	691				691	
		Schwarzburg Sondershausen	451				451	
		Schwarzburg Rudolstadt	539				539	
		Hohenzollern Sigmaringen	356				356	
		Hohenzollern Hechingen	145				145	
		Liechtenstein	55				55	
		Reuss, elder line	223				223	
		Reuss, younger do	522				522	
		Frankfort	693				693	
		Total	11,116				11,116	
		Grand total of army of Confederation	238,721	40,754	21,103	2,915	303,493	592

II. RESERVES AND SUBSTITUTES.

Corps d'armée.	Divisions.	States.	Infantry.	Cavalry.	Artillery and Train.	Pioneers and Pontoniers.	Total.	Guns.
I., II., III., IV., V., VI., VII VIII.	6	Austria	36,750	6,773	3,414	474	47,411	96
	6	Prussia	30,834	5,660	2,852	396	39,742	80
	2	Bavaria	13,793	2,543	1,286	178	17,800	36
	1	Wirtemberg	5,408	997	502	70	6,977	14
	1	Baden	3,876	714	360	50	5,000	10
	1	G. D. Hesse	2,401	443	223	31	3,098	8
		Total of 8th division	11,685	2,154	1,086	151	15,075	32
IX.	1	Saxony	4,651	857	432	60	6,000	12
	1	E. Hessen	2,201	406	204	28	2,839	6
		Nassau	1,860	...	144	15	2,019	4
		Total of 9th division	8,712	1,263	780	103	10,858	22
		Garrison of Luxemburg	990	183	105		1,278	3
X.	1	Hanover	5,060	932	470	75	6,527	14
		Brunswick	813	150	75	10	1,048	2
		Holstein Lauenburg	1,395	257	130	18	1,800	4
	1	Mecklenburg-Schwerin	1,387	256	129	18	1,790	4
		Mecklenburg-Strelitz	293	36	26	4	359	1
		Oldenburg	1,310	...	79	11	1,400	2
		Hamburg	503	93	47	6	649	} 2
	1	Bremen	189	35	17	2	243	
		Lübeck	157	29	15	2	203	
		Total of 10th division	11,107	1,788	988	136	14,019	29
	Reserve Infantry Division.	Saxe-Weimar	1,005				1,005	
		Saxe-Altenburg	491				491	
		Saxe-Coburg-Gotha	583				583	
		Saxe-Meiningen	575				575	
		Anhalt Dessau	265				265	
		Anhalt Bernberg	185				185	
		Anhalt Köthen	163				163	
		Hesse Homburg	100				100	
		Waldeck	259				259	
		Schaumburg Lippe	120				120	
		Lippe	345				345	
		Schwarzburg Sondershausen	226				226	
		Schwarzburg Rudolstadt	269				269	
		Hohenzollern Sigmaringen	178				178	
		Hohenzollern Hechingen	73				73	
		Liechtenstein	28				28	
		Reuss, elder line	112				112	
		Reuss, younger do	261				261	
		Frankfort	346				346	
		Total	5,584				5,584	
		Grand total of Reserve ...	119,455	20,364	10,510	1,438	151,767	298

It is highly probable, however, that the army of confederation, a mere plaything of peace, would be dissolved immediately on the outbreak of a general war. Hence it will be desirable for us to regard the different smaller states of Germany as independent of each other, and give details of the organisation of their armies without reference to the Bund.

THE BAVARIAN ARMY.

The Bavarian army, in its strength, takes the third place among the armies of Germany. It is now sufficiently large to form an independent corps in any war, and, consequently, possesses very considerable importance. The results of the year 1848 have proved highly beneficial to this army. It was not only considerably augmented in that year (each infantry regiment by a battalion, each cavalry regiment by a squadron, and the artillery by a horse regiment), but also greatly reformed. Discipline was more stringently regarded, and considerable attention paid to the education of the officers. The troops were exercised repeatedly and reviewed, and all the manœuvres really of value in war, and not merely for parade, are now kept up sedulously. The unmistakable benefits of all these changes are already very perceptible, and the troops are in a great state of efficiency.

The staff is composed of—

    1 field-marshal.

    4 generals (including 1 master of the ordnance).

11 lieutenant-generals.
32 major-generals.

QUARTERMASTER-GENERAL'S STAFF.

1 quartermaster-general.
1 lieutenant-general.
3 colonels.
2 lieutenant-colonels.
5 majors.
15 captains.

INFANTRY.

The infantry, at the present time, is composed of—

1. Sixteen regiments of the line, each $= 3$ battalions, each battalion $= 6$ companies.   The latter composed of—

4 officers.
2 under-officers.
14 non-commissioned officers.
2 musicians.
2 pioneers.
178 rank and file, or 202 combatants.

The battalion contains—

1 major.
1 adjutant.
1 battalion surgeon.
1 assistant-surgeon.

1 quartermaster.
1 ensign.
1 battalion drummer, and
5 companies, or 1009 combatants.

The whole 48 battalions of the line would, therefore, contain 48,432 men, of whom, during peace,
two-thirds are on furlough. The armament consists
of a percussion musket with bayonet, 24 men in each
company carrying Thouvenin rifles, and, in addition,
all the soldiers have short side-arms. The uniform
consists of trowsers and tunics of light-blue cloth with
various collars and facings, a long gray very good
cloth cloak, and a small low leather casque with a
black woollen crest. The accoutrements are white.

2. Six chasseur battalions, each battalion = 6 companies. Each company is made up of—

4 officers.
14 under-officers.
3 buglers.
2 pioneers.
158 rank and file, or 181 combatants.

The battalion consists of—

1 staff officer.
1 adjutant.
3 surgeons.
7 auditors, quartermasters, &c.
1 ensign.
1 staff bugler, and
5 companies.

Altogether amounting to 909 men; whence the whole body of chasseurs, on a full war footing, would amount to 5454 men. The chasseurs wear the same uniform as the line (except that the collars are light-green), and are now armed with rifles, though, till very recently, there was no distinction, strange to say, between them and the line, although such magnificent shots could be drawn from the Bavarian Alps and the Spessart.

The total strength of the Bavarian infantry consequently amounts to 53,886 men on the full war complement. But as there are no reserves or depôts in Bavaria (the Landwehr forming merely a civic guard), not more than 40,000 could be sent into the field, which is, certainly, a very considerable number for a kingdom like Bavaria.*

CAVALRY.

1. Two regiments of cuirassiers, each regiment of 3 divisions = 6 squadrons (in war a depôt will be established). Each squadron has 4 officers, 16 under-officers, 3 trumpeters, and 135 privates; or, altogether, 158 men. The whole regiment is made up of—

1 colonel.
3 staff officers.
5 surgeons (1 veterinary).
1 regimental adjutant.

* At the time we are writing a very large augmentation is taking place.

9 auditors, gunsmiths, &c.
1 staff trumpeter, and
6 squadrons;

amounting to 956 men; or the two cuirassier regiments, on the full war complement, 1912 men.

The cuirassiers are generally very tall and powerful men, mounted on strong North German horses. Their principal arm is a long, straight sabre, and each man has one pistol. The uniform consists of a light-blue tunic and trowsers with a red stripe, breast and back cuirass of polished steel, steel helmet, and white horseman's mantle; and they are very fine-looking soldiers.

2. Six regiments of chevau-légers of similar strength and formation with the cuirassiers; or, altogether, 36 squadrons on the war footing = 5736 men. They are mounted on native horses very compactly built, wear dark-green tunics with red facings, trowsers of the same colour with broad red stripes, helmet same pattern as infantry, with white plume, and are armed with a sabre and carbine. They are excellent troops, and distinguished themselves greatly in all the campaigns in which the Bavarian troops were engaged.

The total strength of the Bavarian cavalry, without depôts, is, consequently, 7650 men. By great exertions, 7000 of these might be employed in an external campaign.

THE ARTILLERY.

In addition to the ordnance and two laboratory

companies, the artillery is made up of 2 regiments of foot and 1 regiment of horse artillery. Each regiment of foot artillery has 6 batteries of heavy, and 6 batteries of light artillery, each of 8 guns; or, altogether, 96 guns.

A battery or company has, including officers, 133 men. In addition to these 12 companies, each artillery regiment has 3 companies of fortress artillery, altogether amounting to 621 men, and contains altogether, without transport, 2231 men.

The horse artillery regiment has 4 batteries, each of 8 guns, with a total strength of 816 men, including officers, thus made up :—

1 staff officer.
1 adjutant.
3 surgeons.
7 auditors, quartermasters, &c.
1 ensign.
1 staff bugler.
4 companies or batteries.

The total strength of the Bavarian artillery, inclusive of the fortress artillery, laboratory companies, &c., amounts, on a full war complement, to 5642 men, of whom, in case of need, 4100 men, with 224 guns, could march into the field.

The *matériel* of the artillery is excellent, though not particularly elegant. The native horses are small and ugly, but strong and persevering. The uniform consists of dark-blue tunics and trowsers, with black collar and facings, infantry helmets, and dark-gray cloaks.

M

THE ENGINEERS.

In addition to the staff, Bavaria possesses 1 engineer regiment, also performing the duties of pontonniers. It is divided into 8 companies of 127 men, or 1026 combatants, much resembling the artillerymen in dress. The regiment is thus made up:—

1 colonel, 4 staff officers, 2 adjutants, 2 ensigns, 1 staff bugler, 8 companies.

There are also 2 sanitary companies, each containing 5 officers, 1 battalion surgeon, 18 under-officers, 3 buglers, 179 rank and file = 206 men, or together = 412 men.

The total strength of the Bavarian army, in a full war complement, all corps being calculated, will amount to 72,567 men.

In a foreign war might be employed—

Infantry . . .	40,000 men.	
Cavalry . . .	7,000 „	
Artillery . . .	4,100 „	with 224 guns.
Engineers . . .	800 „	
Sanitary companies .	412 „	

Total, 52,312 men, without train.

During peace, the Bavarian army is divided into 2 corps d'armée, each containing 2 divisions of infantry and 1 of cavalry, with the requisite number of guns.

REMARKS.

Service from 21 to 27 in the line, from 27 to 40 in the reserve. In addition, there is a universal Landwehr, with liability to serve up to the 60th year.

THE SAXON ARMY.

This army has also been considerably augmented since 1848, and considerably improved.

THE STAFF.

1 general, 7 lieutenant-generals, 6 major-generals.

ENGINEER DEPARTMENT.

1 colonel
2 staff officers } Engineer division.
2 captains
1 captain (cavalry)
1 ditto (infantry) } Tactical department.
4 first-lieutenants
10 guides.

INFANTRY.

On a war footing, Saxony has 4 infantry brigades and 1 brigade of chasseurs.

1 infantry battalion:—1 staff officer, 1 adjutant, 1 ensign, 1 battalion signalist, 14 officers, 68 under-officers, 16 signalists, 872 rank and file (including 64 tirailleurs), 8 carpenters = 982 combatants.

1 chasseur battalion :—Staff as above, 18 officers, 20 upper chasseurs, 20 signalists, 872 chasseurs, 8 carpenters = 1001 combatants.

1 infantry or chasseur brigade :—1 chief, 1 brigadier (colonel or major-general), 2 adjutants, 1 brigade fourier, 1 brigade signalist, 4 infantry or chasseur battalions = 3933, or 4009 combatants.

The total strength of the Saxon infantry, exclusive of 4 infantry and 1 chasseur battalion as reserve = 20 battalions, with 19,741 combatants, of whom 18,000 could be brought into the field. The Saxon infantry wears a uniform greatly at variance with the other German troops, and not particularly handsome. The tunics are green, with light-blue collars and cuffs, light-blue trowsers, and little low caps after the Austrian pattern. The chasseurs wear dark-green, with black collars. They are armed with percussioned muskets and bayonets ; 2 under-officers and 16 tirailleurs in each company with Minié rifles.

CAVALRY.

Cavalry is composed of 4 light regiments, 1 of the guards, each of 5 squadrons.

1 squadron :—4 officers, 13 under-officers, 3 trumpeters, 138 horsemen = 158 combatants, 154 horses.

1 regiment :—1 colonel, 1 staff officer, 1 adjutant, 1 staff sergeant-major, 1 staff trumpeter, 5 squadrons = 795 combatants, with 772 horses.

Total strength of the cavalry, 3180 combatants, with 3088 horses.

ARTILLERY.

1 foot artillery regiment of 3 brigades or 10 batteries (1 6-pounder, 2 12-pounder, 2 depôt batteries, and 2 principal parks), 1 horse brigade of 2 batteries.

1 ordnance and artisan company, 2 ammunition, 1 chief park, 1 depôt.

The foot artillery regiment (without park and depôt) :—1 colonel, 3 staff officers, 3 adjutants, 6 batteries with 38 guns = 986 combatants.

Brigade of horse artillery :—1 staff officer, 1 adjutant, 2 batteries with 12 guns = 346 combatants.

Total strength of the artillery, without park or depôts = 8 batteries with 50 guns, and 1232 combatants.

PIONEERS.

The pioneer and pontonnier division contains 250 combatants ; the pontoon train, on a war complement, 225 men, with 408 horses.

The commissariat train company contains 3 officers and 559 men.

SANITARY COMPANY.

Sanitary company is made up of 4 officers, 19 under-officers, 3 signalists, 220 men.

The total strength of the Saxon troops, without reserves and depôts, will amount to 24,750 combatants, with 50 guns, of whom about 20,000 could be employed in an external campaign.

REMARKS.—Six years' service, with substitution, three years' reserve. Usually but a small proportion of the army is called out.

THE HANOVERIAN ARMY.

STAFF.

1 field-marshal, 1 general, 8 lieutenant-generals, 10 major-generals.

GENERAL STAFF.

1 lieutenant-general as chief, 2 staff officers, 1 captain, 7 officers.

INFANTRY.

8 infantry regiments (1 guards and 1 corps de garde), each of 2 battalions or 8 companies, 1 guards chasseur battalion, 3 light battalions of 4 companies.

1 line or light infantry company:—5 officers, 14 under-officers, 3 musicians, 188 rank and file (10 tirailleurs) = 210 combatants.

1 battalion:—1 lieutenant-colonel, 1 major, 1 adjutant, 1 staff ensign, 1 battalion drummer, 4 companies = 845 combatants.

1 regiment:—1 colonel, 1 staff officer, 1 staff ensign, 1 staff fourier, 6 musicians, 2 battalions = 1700 combatants.

1 light battalion:—1 lieutenant-colonel, 1 major, 1 adjutant, 1 staff ensign, 1 staff fourier, 1 battalion bugler, 3 musicians, 4 companies = 849 combatants.

Total strength of the infantry, without reserves (120 men to each battalion), 20 battalions, or about 17,000 effectives.

The infantry are equipped and dressed exactly after the Prussian model. In the line, the under-officers and tirailleurs have Thouvenin rifles with bayonets; the remainder, muskets. All the light infantry are armed with rifles.

CAVALRY.

6 regiments (1 garde du corps), 1 guard cuirassiers, 2 hussar (1 guards), 2 dragoon regiments, each of 4 squadrons.

1 squadron :—5 officers, 14 non-commissioned officers, 4 trumpeters, 117 men = 150 combatants.

1 regiment:—1 commandant, 1 staff officer, 1 adjutant, 1 staff sergeant-major, 1 staff orderly, 4 squadrons = 605 combatants.

Total strength of the cavalry, 3630 combatants.

The Hanoverian cavalry certainly possess the best *matériel* to be found in Germany. The horses, all reared at home, are excellent. The men are voluntary recruits from the peasant classes, who sign an agreement for eight years. When they go on furlough during that period, they take their horses with them.

ARTILLERY (ENGLISH PATTERN).

1 artillery brigade, containing 2 companies of horse artillery, 2 battalions or 7 companies of foot artillery,

and a laboratory company. The two horse companies contain 2 horse batteries, the 7 foot companies 3 9-pounder batteries and 16-pounder battery, as well as 1 siege park, 1 ammunition column, and 1 depôt company.

Staff of the artillery brigade : — 1 major-general, 5 staff officers, 4 adjutants, 1 staff pyrotechnist, 8 gunners.

A 6-pounder foot battery :—5 officers, 19 non-commissioned officers, 3 trumpeters, 116 gunners = 173 combatants.

A 9-pounder foot battery :—5 officers, 19 non-commissioned officers, 3 buglers, 165 gunners = 192 combatants.

A horse battery :—5 officers, 19 non-commissioned officers, 3 buglers, 118 gunners = 175 combatants.

Total strength of the artillery, 6 batteries with 36 guns, and 1118 combatants.

ENGINEER CORPS.

Cadre :—staff, with pioneer and pontonnier company.

1 company :—4 officers, 8 under-officers, 2 buglers, 83 men = 97 combatants.

The corps without reserve :—1 colonel, 1 staff officer, 1 adjutant, 197 men, and 1 Birago pontoon train.

Total strength of the Hanoverian troops, without reserve, about 22,000 men, with 36 guns, of whom 18,000 could be employed in an external campaign.*

* The infantry has been recently greatly augmented.

THE WIRTEMBERG TROOPS.

GENERAL STAFF.

6 lieutenant-generals, 10 major-generals.

QUARTERMASTER-GENERAL'S STAFF.

1 major-general, 1 staff officer, 6 captains, 7 lieutenants.

ENGINEER CORPS.

1 colonel, 1 staff officer (belonging to quartermaster-general's staff), 6 captains, 2 lieutenants.

PIONEER COMPANY.

INFANTRY.

8 regiments of 2 battalions or 8 companies, with a disciplinary company.

1 company:—4 officers, 21 non-commissioned officers, 3 musicians, 195 men (including 2 carpenters and 36 tirailleurs) = 223 combatants.

1 battalion:—1 battalion commandant, 1 staff officer, 1 adjutant, 1 rifle officer, 1 battalion drummer, 4 companies = 897 combatants.

1 regiment:—1 regimental commandant, 1 adjutant, 1 staff fourier, 2 battalions = 1797 combatants.

Total strength of the infantry, 14,376 effectives.

The infantry are armed with percussioned muskets

and bayonets, the tirailleurs with rifles.   The buglers
also carry muskets.

CAVALRY.

1 squadron of guards, 4 cavalry regiments of 4
squadrons, and 1 courier division (army police).

1 squadron :—4 officers, 24 non-commissioned officers, 4 trumpeters, 138 men = 170 combatants.

1 regiment:—1 regimental commandant, 1 staff officer, 1 adjutant, 1 rifle officer, 1 staff trumpeter, 1 staff
fourier, 4 squadrons = 680 combatants.

Total strength of cavalry, 18 squadrons = 2949
combatants.   They are armed with carbines, sabres,
and pistols.   They are tall, powerful men, and their
horses, which contain a great admixture of Arab
blood, appear too light for them.

ARTILLERY.

The regiment of artillery is divided into 2 horse
battalions with 7 batteries.

1 battery :—4 officers, 18 non-commissioned officers,
16 upper-gunners, 4 trumpeters or buglers, 117 gunners, 2 officers, 7 to 8 non-commissioned officers, 79
to 85 train soldiers = 250 combatants.

Total strength of the artillery, 7 batteries with 42
guns, and 1764 combatants.

The guns are principally 12-pounders and 10-
pounder howitzers, and are excellently worked in the
field.

PIONEERS.

1 pioneer company of 4 officers and 171 men = 175 men.

Total strength of the troops, 19,000, with 42 guns, of whom 16,000 infantry and 2500 cavalry could be employed in the field.

REMARKS.—Six years' service, with substitution; liability to serve in the three bans of the Landwehr till attaining 32 years of age.

THE TROOPS OF BADEN.

INFANTRY.

1 grenadier and 3 line infantry regiments, each of 2 battalions or 8 companies, with 1929 effectives; 2 fusilier battalions, each of 4 companies, or 970 combatants; 1 chasseur battalion of 3 companies, with 532 effectives = 10,223 men, without depôt.

CAVALRY.

3 regiments of 4 squadrons, each of 800 men = 2451 men.

ARTILLERY.

1 regiment of 4 foot batteries and 1 horse battery = 40 guns, with 1700 men.

PIONEERS.

1 company of pioneers, with 1 Birago pontoon service and 255 men; 1 company of ordnance workmen.

Total strength of the Baden troops = 15,000 men, with 40 guns, of whom about 13,000 could be employed in the field. Since the catastrophe of 1849, these troops have been entirely re-organised, and are now on the Prussian model.

REMARKS.—Six years' service, two of them in the reserve : substitution.

THE TROOPS OF ELECTORAL HESSE.

(PRUSSIAN PATTERN.)

INFANTRY.

4 regiments (1 guards), each of 1543 men, in 2 battalions or 8 companies, 1 chasseur battalion of 110, and 1 fusilier battalion of 711 effectives = 7301 combatants.

CAVALRY.

2 Hessian regiments of 7 squadrons, 1028 effectives; 2 squadrons of cuirassiers (in peace, 1 division garde du corps instead), with 300 combatants; 18 men army gensdarmerie = 1350 combatants.

ARTILLERY.

1 regiment of 2 6-pounder foot batteries and 1 horse battery; 1 ammunition column = 718 men; 1 pioneer company with 94 men = 812 combatants.

Total strength of the Electoral troops, 11,800 men, with three batteries or 19 guns, of whom about 10,000 could be sent into the field.

REMARKS. — Service from the twentieth to the thirtieth year, in two levies: substitution.

THE TROOPS OF HESSE-DARMSTADT.

(PRUSSIAN PATTERN.)

INFANTRY :—2 brigades = 4 regiments, or 8 battalions of 3 companies = 8041 men.

CAVALRY :—1 regiment chevaux-légers, of 3 divisions or 6 squadrons = 1404 men.

ARTILLERY :—2 companies of foot artillery of 12 guns, 1 company of horse artillery of 6 guns, 1 company of artillery train = 847 men.

PIONEERS :—1 company, with half a pontoon train, and about 120 men.

Total strength of the Hesse-Darmstadt troops,

10,498 men, with 18 guns, of whom about 9000 could take the field.

REMARKS.—Six years' service, with substitution; two of them reserve.

NASSAU.

INFANTRY :—7 battalions of 4 companies = 6745 men.

ARTILLERY :—2 companies of 516 men, and 12 guns.

PIONEERS :—56 men.

Total strength, 7317 men, with 12 guns.

REMARKS.—Six years' service, with substitution.

BRUNSWICK.

(PRUSSIAN PATTERN, BLACK UNIFORM.)

INFANTRY :—1 regiment of 2 line and 2 Landwehr battalions, 1 battalion of guards.

CAVALRY :—1 regiment of hussars of 2 squadrons, and 2 squadrons Landwehr.

Together amounting to 4857 men.

ARTILLERY :—302 men, with 12 guns.

Total strength, 5359 men, with 12 guns (including the entire militia).

REMARKS. — Seven years' service, including two years' reserve: substitution.

MECKLENBURG-SCHWERIN.

(PRUSSIAN PATTERN).

INFANTRY :—1 grenadier battalion of 4 companies, 965 men; 2 musketeer battalions of 4 companies, 1866 men ; 1 light battalion of 4 companies, 628 men.

CAVALRY :—1 regiment of 4 squadrons, and 629 men.

ARTILLERY AND PIONEERS :—654 men, with 16 guns.

Total strength, 4752 men, with 16 guns.

REMARKS.—Six years' service : substitution.

MECKLENBURG-STRELITZ.

(PRUSSIAN PATTERN).

INFANTRY : — 1 battalion of 4 companies = 718 men, and 359 men reserve.

OLDENBURG

(PRUSSIAN PATTERN).

INFANTRY :—4 battalions of 5 companies (including 1 rifle company) = 2280 men.

CAVALRY :—3 squadrons = 410 men.

ARTILLERY :—2 companies of 369 men, and 16 guns ; 14 men ordnance.

Total strength, 3673 men, with 16 guns (including reserve).

REMARKS.—Six years' service : substitution.

THE SAXON PRINCIPALITIES.

The contingents of the Principalities are made up exclusively of infantry, and form the so-called " reserve division" of the German Federal Army, although it is probable this arrangement would be destroyed in case of a general war.   Since 1848 these contingents have been greatly improved, by introducing Prussian organisation.   The colour of the uniform is green, but otherwise they bear a great resemblance to the Prussian soldiers.

The several contingents are :—

SAXE-WEIMAR.—2 battalions of infantry of about

1000 men on the war establishment. In case of
need, a third battalion (reserve) of 1000 men can be
formed.

SAXE-COBURG GOTHA.—2 battalions of infantry
= 1266 men, to which may be added, in case of need,
a reserve battalion of 800 men. The total strength,
on a war complement, would therefore be about 3300
men.

SAXE-MEININGEN.—1 battalion of 5 companies on
a war footing = 1142 men.

SAXE-ALTENBURG.—1 battalion on a war footing,
including reserve, about 1400 men. In case of a
foreign war, these four Saxon Duchies could furnish
an infantry corps of from 6000 to 7000 men.

The three Anhalt Principalities bring into the
field about 4000 men, including reserve, divided into
3 battalions, and re-organised since 1849 entirely on
the Prussian model.

The two Principalities of Reuss, including reserve,
about 900 men, in 1 battalion.

The two Principalities of Schwartzburg-Rudolstadt
and Sondershausen together, including reserve, about
1500 men.

The Principality of Waldeck, 1 battalion of 800
men, among them excellent riflemen.

The Principalities of Lippe Ditmold and Schaum-
burg, including reserve, about 1300 men.

The Principality of Lichtenstein, including reserve, about 83 men.

The Landgraviate of Hesse-Homburg, including reserve, about 350 men, in 2 companies.

The total strength of all these contingents, forming the reserve division, including reserves and depôts, would amount to 16,000 men, about 12,000 of whom could be employed in a foreign campaign. They are excellently drilled, and in a good state of efficiency.

The free towns, Hamburg, Lübeck, Bremen, and Frankfort, have the only contingents in Germany composed of volunteers. They furnish about 3500 men, infantry, including reserve, and 469 dragoons. They are after the Prussian pattern, and excellent troops, as they are principally soldiers who have served their time in other armies.

We have purposely omitted the contingents which Holland and Denmark should furnish to the German Army of Confederation. Either those kingdoms would unite with Germany, and then bring their entire armies into the field, or, in the other case, they would hold back their contingents. In 1848 and 1849 Holland did not send a single man to take part in the Schleswig-Holstein campaign, though portions of even the smallest German contingents were obliged to march. It would be absurd to calculate on any assistance from Denmark, where the soldiers are severely punished for evincing the slightest feeling of partiality for Germany.

If we recapitulate the strength of all the troops of the various states which they could furnish at short notice for a foreign campaign, without weakening the necessary garrisons, depôts, and reserves at home, we shall have the following satisfactory result:—

State.	Infantry.	Cavalry.	Engineers, &c.	Guns.
Bavaria......................	40,000	7,000	5,300	200
Saxony	15,000	3,000	2,000	50
Hanover	13,000	3,000	2,000	36
Wirtemberg................	12,000	2,500	1,500	42
Baden	10,000	2,200	1,400	40
Hesse-Cassel................	8,000	1,100	900	18
Hesse-Darmstadt.........	7,300	1,100	900	18
Nassau	6,000	...	450	12
Mecklenburg-Schwerin .	3,000	600	550	16
„ Strelitz ...	700			
Oldenburg..................	2,500	400	450	16
Brunswick...................	3,000	580	400	12
Saxe-Weimar............. ⎫				
„ Coburg Gotha ... ⎬	6,500			
„ Meiningen				
„ Altenburg......... ⎭				
Anhalt Dessau.......... ⎫				
„ Köthen .... ⎬	2,000			
„ Bernburg .... ⎭				
Principalities of Reuss..	800			
„ Schwartzburg	1,200			
The two Ditmolds.......	1,000			
Waldeck....................	800			
Hesse-Homburg	400			
The four Hanse Towns .	3,000	400		
TOTAL..........	136,200	21,880	15,850	460

Without taking into calculation the requisite train.

IX.

THE ARMIES AND NAVIES

OF

SWEDEN AND NORWAY.

THE SWEDISH ARMY.

COMMAND IN CHIEF AND GENERAL STAFF.

THE former contains, at the present moment, 24 generals (exclusive of 9 adjutant-generals), of whom, however, only 10 are fit for active service : the latter consists of 60 officers of all grades, who have previously passed an examination.

ENGINEER CORPS.

1 general as chief, 1 colonel, 1 lieutenant-colonel, 2 majors, 8 captains, 9 first-lieutenants, 6 second-lieutenants, several supernumerary lieutenants, and 12 non-commissioned officers.

The topographic works are carried on by a special topographic corps, consisting of 1 colonel (chief), 1 lieutenant-colonel, 1 major, 5 or 6 captains, and 3 first-lieutenants, and is incorporated with the general staff.

As there are no actual engineer troops, the works are carried out by troops of the line, specially attached and formed into companies during a war.

I. RECRUITED TROOPS (VÄR FRADE).

Infantry. { 1 regiment guards, of 2 battalions, or 6 companies.
{ 1 chasseur regiment, of 6 companies (Wärmeland).

Cavalry. { 1 regiment horse guards, of 5 squadrons.
{ 1   „   hussars (Crown Prince), of 8 squadrons.

Artillery. { 3 regiments, of which 2 are mixed horse and foot ;
{   1 regiment horse artillery.
{ 1 pyrotechnic corps, for the rocket brigade.

1 regiment "Swea artillery" = 6 field batteries, ⎫ With 6
    and 1 foot battery.   ⎬ depôt
1 regiment "Götha artillery" = 6 field batteries. ⎭ companies.

1   „   "Wendes artillery" = 4 horse bat- ⎧ With 2
    teries.   ⎨ depôt
                                               ⎩ companies.

Each of the two first regiments contains 4 6-pounder batteries, 1 12-pounder and 1 24-pounder battery.

The 3d regiment contains 3 6-pounder batteries and 1 12-pounder battery.

A 6-pounder battery = 6 6-pounder guns, and 2 ⎞ = 8 guns
    12-pounder howitzers.   ⎟ per
A 12-pounder battery = 8 12-pounder guns.   ⎬ battery.
A 24-   „   „   = 8 24-   „   „   ⎠

Strength of the Värfrade, 7692 men, with 136 guns.

II. INCORPORATED TROOPS (INDELTA).

INFANTRY. — 20 regiments of 2 battalions, or 8 companies and 5 independent battalions (the " Smaland " regiment has only 1 battalion of 4 companies).

CAVALRY. — 6 regiments, varying from 1 to 8 squadrons.

(Each province has 1 Indelta regiment to which it gives its name).

Strength of the Indelta troops = 33,400 men.

III. RESERVE OR CONSCRIPTION TROOPS (BEVAERINS).

Total strength = 95,300 men.

The entire reserve of the army has 404 officers.

IV. THE GOTHLAND MILITIA.

21 companies, with 90 officers, 70 non-commissioned officers, 63 musicians, 7621 men (belonging to the standing army), with 16 guns.

Total strength of the Swedish army, about 144,000 men, with 152 guns.

The whole army is armed with percussion muskets.

REMARKS.—The first mentioned troops are enlisted for at least 3, at most 12 years, but on the average for 8 years.

Organisation of the Indelta troops.—Each soldier receives a piece of land (Torp) large enough for himself and family, either from a landed proprietor, or from the Crown, which has special estates allotted for the purpose. In addition, each soldier, on entering, receives a bounty of from 10 to 30 R. Thaler Bco., besides annual pay of small amount from the owners of the land. The state provides the equipment, &c., but, with the exception of the cloak, the landlords must pay half the expense. The engagement with the soldiers, by which the landowner is freed from personal military duties, generally lasts as long as he is fit for service. The officers of the Indelta troops are also settled on the crown lands in the middle of their districts, and their pay is made up by the state. These troops are annually exercised for four weeks in companies, battalions, and regiments, during which period they receive actual pay. The conscription troops are chosen from all Swedes capable of bearing arms, between the ages of 20 and 25, and are divided into five classes. After they have been thoroughly disciplined, a battalion per regiment is called out annually during peace for a fortnight's exercise.

THE SWEDISH NAVY.

PERSONNEL OF THE FLEET.

1 admiral, 2 vice-admirals, 5 rear-admirals, 200 captains and lieutenants, 1850 marine artillerymen, sailors, and boys, 1540 pilots, artisans, &c., 8200 boatmen, 1160 seebeverings (boats' crews), 34 companies marines (royal fleet), 15 companies marines (gun-boat flotilla), 30 companies Indelta sailors.

To these must be added the sailors raised by conscription, which will bring up the personnel to about 24,000 men.

FLEET.

12 ships of the line, 8 frigates, 8 brigs and corvettes, 6 schooners, 8 mortar vessels, 22 transport ships, 256 gun-boats, and 12 steamers. Total, 332 vessels.

THE NORWEGIAN ARMY.

THIS army is organised very differently from the Swedish, and is under an entirely separate administration.

GENERAL STAFF.

The Norwegian army has a command-in-chief, composed of 2 lieutenant-generals and 8 major-generals, with 1 adjutant-general. The general staff has the following strength :—1 chief, who must be a colonel at the least, 2 lieutenant-colonels, or higher officers, 1 major, all permanent members ; 3 adjutants of the first class, and 3 do. second class, who are all captains or lieutenants of the army, as general officers ; 1 secretary and accountant, 3 staff-fouriers, and 2 staff-sergeants.

ARMY.

INFANTRY :—5 brigades, of which the 1st and 2d have four, the 3d, 4th, and 5th, three battalions, altogether amounting to 11,924 men.

A peculiar corps in the Norwegian infantry is formed of several companies of skielöbere or skaters, acting as light infantry, armed with rifles and sticks 7 feet long.

CAVALRY.

1 brigade of 3 chasseur corps = 1070 men.

ARTILLERY.

1 artillery regiment with a strength of 1330 men.

If we add the reserve of 9160 men, the strength of the Norwegian army will amount to about 23,500 men.

THE NORWEGIAN NAVY.

PERSONNEL OF THE FLEET.

1 vice-admiral.
1 commander.
3 commander-captains.
24 captains.
48 lieutenants.
350 petty officers and marines.
1 shipbuilding company of 180 men.
1 artillery   do.   ⎫
1 laboratory   do.   ⎬ 360 do.
1 artisan   do.   ⎭

Altogether there are about 30,000 enrolled sailors between the ages of 30 and 60 years.

FLEET.

2 frigates, 1 corvette, 1 brig, 5 schooners, 4 steamers, 136 gun-boats.

Total strength of the united Swedish and Norwegian armies = 167,500 men, with, at least, 152 guns.

X.

DANISH ARMY AND NAVY.

THE DANISH ARMY.

COMMAND-IN-CHIEF. — 2 generals, 5 lieutenant-generals, 12 major-generals.

GENERAL STAFF.—1 general as chief, 4 staff officers, 5 captains.

INFANTRY.

23 battalions, of 4 companies, or 4 brigades =
{ 1 battalion life guards.
12 „ line infantry.
5 „ light „
5 chasseur corps. } = 16,630 men (peace establishment).

1 company = 4 officers, 26 non-commissioned officers, 148 drummers and men.

Armament :—The line infantry carry percussioned muskets with bayonet, excepting 16 men per company, who, like the chasseur corps, are armed with rifles.

O

CAVALRY.

27 squadrons, or 3 brigades. { 3 squadrons of horse guards (1 life guard squadron, and the guard hussar division.) 3 regiments dragoons, of 4 squadrons. } = 2895 men.

1 squadron = 4 officers, 20 non-commissioned officers, 115 buglers and men.

ARTILLERY.

1 brigade of 2 regiments, or 12 batteries and 1 arsenal company. } = 2560 men, with 96 guns.

These consist of 2 12-pounder and 10 6-pounder batteries, each of 6 guns and 2 howitzers.

1 battery = 4 officers, with 208 non-commissioned officers and men.

1 regiment = 1 general, 6 staff officers, 24 officers, 1272 non-commissioned officers and men, as effectives.

ENGINEER CORPS.

1 general engineer chief, 3 colonels, 24 majors, and 24 officers, 2 companies of engineers, and 1 pioneer company, each of 110 men. } = 362 men.

Total strength of the Danish army on a peace establishment = about 22,900. Of these the following form the so-called German contingent for Holstein

Lauenburg. 2791 men, line, infantry, and chasseurs; 514 cavalry; 259 men, artillery, with 8 guns; 36 pioneers and pontonniers; or, altogether, exclusive of 1800 men substitution and reserve = 3600 men.

The war establishment of the Danish army is, however, considerably larger, as, by calling in the reserves, the squadrons can be raised to 180 men, the companies to 200, and the engineers and artillery equivalently augmented. At the same time, 32 reserve battalions, 24 reserve squadrons, and 6 6-pounder light batteries can be called out. Before the outbreak of the last war, Denmark had 49,301 infantry, 10,627 cavalry, 8153 artillerymen, with 144 guns, and 847 engineers; or, altogether, about 69,000 men, who, in case of need, could now be augmented to between 90,000 and 100,000 men.

REMARKS.—The time of serving in the active army is 8 years, commencing from the age of 22 (ballot). Of those years, 4 in the line and 2 in the artillery are counted to the reserve. From the 38th year a second 8 years of service commences, in the first levy, and then service in the reserve till the 45th year is attained.

THE DANISH NAVY.

PERSONNEL OF THE FLEET.

1 vice-admiral, 2 rear-admirals, 8 commandants, 8 captains commandant, 17 captains, 26 captain lieutenants, 41 first-lieutenants, 36 second-lieutenants, 2 commander lieutenants, 10 captains and captain lieutenants.

2 divisions, with 1975 gunners, sailors, boys, artisans, &c.

At the end of 1853, the number of men in the service amounted to about 30,000, of whom Schleswig and Holstein furnished from 1-4th to 1-3rd.

FLEET.

5 ships of the line.	3 of 84 guns	=	252 guns.		
	1 „ 80 „	=	80 „		
	1 „ 66 „	=	66 „		
9 frigates.	1 „ 60 „	=	60 „		
	1 „ 48 „	=	48 „		
	4 „ 46 „	=	184 „		
	1 „ 44 „	=	44 „		
	2 „ 40 „	=	80 „		
4 corvettes.	1 „ 28 „	=	28 „		
	3 „ 20 „	=	60 „		
1 bark	„ 14 „	=	14 „		
4 brigs.	2 „ 16 „	=	32 „		
	2 „ 12 „	=	24 „		
3 schooners.	1 „ 8 „	=	8 „		
	2 „ 1 „	=	2 „		
3 cutters.	1 „ 2 „	=	6 „	} Falconets.	
	2 „ 2 „	=	4 „		

6 steamers, together, of 1120 horse-power, with 35 guns, of them 1 of 260, 1 of 200, 1 of 160 horse-power.

Total—35 ships, with 1017 guns, and 1120 horse-power. To this amount we must add the rowing flotilla of 23 bomb-shallops, 47 gun-boats, and 47 bomb-yawls.

XI.

THE BELGIAN ARMY.

THE BELGIAN ARMY.

COMMAND-IN-CHIEF :—12 lieutenant-generals, 20 major-generals.

GENERAL STAFF : — 3 colonels, 3 lieutenant-colonels, 4 majors, 40 subaltern officers.

(This is exclusive of the provincial and fortress staff, who together amount to 26 commandants and 36 adjutants).

Since the year 1853, the officers of the Belgian army, including staff officers, have been divided into 2 sections: active and reserve. In the latter, there are only 2 lieutenant-generals and 4 major-generals at the present time.

INFANTRY.

16 regiments, 1 of them carbineers, of 4 battalions, or 24 companies, amounting to 3672 men, and 2 regiments of chasseurs au pied of 3 battalions or 18

companies, amounting to 2800 men. In addition, there belong to the infantry 1 non-commissioned officer sedentary company of 70, and 1 fusilier sedentary company of 124 men; each regiment has 1 reserve battalion of 6 companies.

Armament — Line: — Minié percussioned guns. Chasseurs:—percussioned rifles with sword bayonet.

Strength of the infantry without reserves = about 46,000 men.

CAVALRY.

7 regiments as follow:—2 regiments chasseurs à cheval of 6 squadrons with 913 men, 2 regiments of lancers, and 1 regiment guides, of the same strength, 2 regiments cuirassiers of 4 squadrons with 619 men. Each regiment has a reserve squadron attached to it.

Strength of cavalry without reserves = about 5800 men.

ARTILLERY.

4 regiments artillery, 4 companies artillery train, 1 company artillery artisans, 1 company gunsmiths.

1 artillery regiment = 4 mounted batteries with 840 men, 6 fortress batteries with 840 men.

2–4 artillery regiments = 15 field batteries, with 3582 men, 18 fortress companies with 824 men.

Each regiment has 1 depôt battery.

Strength of the artillery = about 7700 men, with 152 guns.

The artillery train amounts to 360, the pontonnier company to 174, the laboratory company to 82, and the company of gunsmiths to 194 men.

ENGINEERS.

1 regiment of 2 battalions or 10 companies, each amounting to 169 men. The general staff contains 3 colonels, 5 lieutenant-colonels, 5 majors, 67 subaltern officers. The regiment, consequently, has a strength of 1690 men.

The Belgian gensdarmerie amounts to 9 companies, with a strength of 1408 men and 1065 horses : there are also 1 company of sons of soldiers, and 1 disciplinary division.

The total strength of the Belgian army, without reserves, would, consequently, amount to about 62,000 men, with 152 guns. Including reserves, it can, according to the recent organisation, be raised to 100,000 men.

REMARKS.—Universal conscription, with ballot, and substitution for 8 years ; of which, however, the half may be estimated as spent on furlough.

THE BELGIAN NAVY

is very insignificant. It contains 1 20-gun brig,
" Duke of Brabant;" 1 goelette of 12 guns, " Louis
Marie;" 2 gun-boats of 5 guns; 3 steamers.

XII.

THE DUTCH ARMY AND NAVY.

THE DUTCH ARMY.

GENERAL COMMAND.

1 field-marshal, 1 general, 5 lieutenant-generals, 13 major-generals.

THE ARMY.

The general staff, local staff, and military administration amount to 1 general, 169 staff and field officers.

INFANTRY.

Staff:—1 major-general as inspector, 5 major-generals (generals of brigade), and 24 officers; 9 regiments, 1 instructing battalion, 1 disciplinary battalion as follows:—

1 regiment grenadiers and chasseurs, in 4 battalions = 3631 men.

8 line regiments, of 4 battalions, or 20 companies; with 1 depôt, each regiment comprising 4925 men. $\Big\} = 39,400$ men.

1 instructing battalion of 4 companies = 410 men.
1 disciplinary depôt of 2 companies = 134 men.
1 colonial dockyard depôt of 2 companies = 240 men.

Armament :—percussioned smooth and rifled muskets, with bayonet.

Total strength of the infantry = 43,860 men.

CAVALRY.

Staff:—1 lieutenant-general as inspector, 2 major-generals (commandants of brigades), 5 officers.

4 dragoon regiments of 5 squadrons (one of them depôt), each of 943 men = 3772 sabres.
1 regiment chasseurs à cheval of 2 squadrons = 625 men.
2 squadrons maréchaussée, or watchmen.

Total strength of the cavalry = 4405 men.

ARTILLERY.

Staff: — 1 general as inspector, 2 directors of artillery, 68 officers, 58 men; 5 regiments artillery (1 regiment field artillery, 3 regiments fortress artillery, 1 regiment horse artillery), 1 corps pontonniers.

1 regiment field artillery=12 com-⎫ = 11 batteries
panies (including 1 depôt), of ⎬ of 8 guns
2560 men. ⎭ each.

3 regiments fortress artillery, each = 13 companies
(1 depôt), with 1784 men.

1 regiment horse artillery = 5 companies (1 depôt),
with 745 men = 4 batteries of 6 guns each.

The pontonnier corps = 212 men.

Total strength of the artillery = about 9030 men.

ENGINEERS.

This arm, in addition to the staff, contains 1 battalion sappers and miners, in 3 companies = 748 men.

Total strength of the Dutch army = about 51,600 men, with 120 guns.

COLONIAL TROOPS.

Holland possesses several regiments in Borneo, Sumatra, Java, &c., which are composed partly of Europeans, partly of natives, but generally of very undisciplined elements, as volunteers, convicts, &c.

Volunteer officers who have served for eight years are relieved at the expiration of that period, and gain a step.

REMARKS.—5 years' service, with ballot and substitution, commencing with the 20th year. The nucleus of the army consists of recruited troops, while the conscripts are discharged as militia at the end of a few months, and are only exercised for a few weeks annually. In addition, there is a reserve (schutters or rifles), which is only embodied in time of war. It is divided into 3 levies, and contains all persons capable of bearing arms, from the 25th to the 35th year. The first levy is composed of 53 battalions, line and artillery ; the second of 29. The state during peace only finds arms and accoutrements, nor is any exception made during the fortnight's annual manœuvres.

THE DUTCH NAVY.

PERSONNEL OF THE FLEET.

1 admiral.
3 vice-admirals.
4 rear-admirals.
20 captains of the line.
30 captains of frigates.
281 lieutenants, first and second class.
149 cadets.
80 surgeons, &c.
64 pursers, &c.
6607 marines (including 520 native Indians).
2 divisions marine infantry of 1524 men.

FLEET.

2 ships of the line of   84 guns.
3 ,,   ,,   74 ,,
5 frigates, first class, of 54 to 60 ,,
8   ,,   second class, 38 ,, 44   ,,
2 frigates (rasee) of 28 guns.
12 corvettes of 18 to 28   ,,
13 brigs,   12 to 18   ,,
21 goelettes,   8 ,,
21 war steamers.
2 transports.
2 frigates,   ⎫
1 corvette,   ⎬ port-ships, with 100 guns.
             ⎭

Altogether = 92 vessels, with 2000 guns; and in addition 49 gun-yawls, with 174 guns.

TABULAR STATEMENT OF THE FORCES ABOVE DESCRIBED.

STATES.	LAND FORCES.					TOTAL.		NAVY.			TOTAL.		
	Infantry.	Cavalry.	Artillery.	Engineers.	Other Troops.	Men.	Guns.	Ships of the Line.	Frigates.	Smaller Vessels.	Ships.	Guns.	Horse-power.
(1.) England..........	119,000	13,600	15,122	2,460	80,000 militia.)	230,200 *	120	94	99	185	371	15,234	54,354
(2.) France	382,000	86,000	57,000	8,900	33,800 (including 25,000 gensdarmerie.)	556,000	1,182	60	78	273	411	11,773†	40,270
(3.) Russia	540,000	80,000	44,000	12,000	473,000	1,154,000	2,250	54	48	84 350 gun-boats.	186 350 gun-boats.	9,000	..
(4.) Turkey..........	100,800	17,280	13,000	1,600	385,000	457,680	360	10	7	60	77	3,000	..
(5.) Sardinia.........	31,900	5,700	4,300	1,159	5,200	47,600	80	1	4	24	29	405	1,690
(6.) Austria	457,000	67,000	47,000	16,800	5,200 (with 1 train.)	593,000	1,140	..	6	98 (including gun-boats.)	104	781	..
(7.) Prussia	372,600	67,600	60,100	7,740	72,700 (including 45,000 train, &c.)	580,800	932	..	1	51 (including gun-boats.)	33	192	..
(8.) Germany	166,000	25,000	14,500	2,027	17,000	224,600	500	..	..	..	..	..	..
Total of 6, 7, 8....	995,600	159,600	131,600	26,600	94,900	1,398,400	2,572	..	7	149	156	973	..
(9.) Sweden and Norway	163,500		4,030		..	167,500	200	12	10	70 399 gun-boats.	92 392 gun-boats.	..	..
(10.) Denmark	50,000	10,600	8,000	850	..	69,000	144	5	9	21 878 gun-boats.	35 87 gun-boats.	1,017	1,120
(11.) Belgium	46,000	5,800	7,700	1,690	..	62,000	152	..	..	5 2 gun-boats.	5 2 gun-boats.	49	..
(12.) Holland..........	43,550	4,400	9,000	748	..	57,700	120	5	15	72 49 gun-boats.	92 49 gun-boats.	9,174	..

* East Indian Army = 348,000, including 31,000 Queen's troops.
† The guns of 121 steamers are not contained in this amount.
The armies of Sardinia, Denmark, Belgium, and Holland, could be largely augmented in case of a war.

For EU product safety concerns, contact us at Calle de José Abascal, 56–1°, 28003 Madrid, Spain or eugpsr@cambridge.org.

www.ingramcontent.com/pod-product-compliance
Ingram Content Group UK Ltd.
Pitfield, Milton Keynes, MK11 3LW, UK
UKHW010338140625
459647UK00010B/674